Crash Course in Disaster Preparedness

Recent Titles in Libraries Unlimited Crash Course Series

Crash Course in Disaster Preparedness

Carmen Cowick

Crash Course

LIBRARIES UNLIMITED™
An Imprint of ABC-CLIO, LLC
Santa Barbara, California • Denver, Colorado

Library of Congress Cataloging-in-Publication Data

Names: Cowick, Carmen, 1981– author.
Title: Crash course in disaster preparedness / Carmen Cowick.
Description: Santa Barbara, California : Libraries Unlimited, 2018. | Series: Crash course | Includes bibliographical references and index.
Identifiers: LCCN 2018019356 (print) | LCCN 2018020982 (ebook) | ISBN 9781440860522 (ebook) | ISBN 9781440860515 (paperback)
Subjects: LCSH: Library buildings—Safety measures—Planning. | Emergency management—Planning. | Library materials—Conservation and restoration—Planning. | Libraries—Information technology—Security measures—Planning.
Classification: LCC Z679.7 (ebook) | LCC Z679.7 .C68 2018 (print) | DDC 025.8/2—dc23
LC record available at https://lccn.loc.gov/2018019356

ISBN: 978-1-4408-6051-5 (paperback)
        978-1-4408-6052-2 (ebook)

22 21 20 19 18   1 2 3 4 5

This book is also available as an eBook.

Libraries Unlimited
An Imprint of ABC-CLIO, LLC

ABC-CLIO, LLC
130 Cremona Drive, P.O. Box 1911
Santa Barbara, California 93116-1911
www.abc-clio.com

This book is printed on acid-free paper ∞

Manufactured in the United States of America

CONTENTS

CHAPTER 1

Introduction to Disaster Planning

INTRODUCTION

Disasters are not a matter of if it will happen to your institution, but rather when it will happen to your institution. Unfortunately, disasters are inevitable, and that is why the planning for such an occurrence needs to be done well ahead of time so that sufficient training can be carried out and the response to the disaster can be swift and effective. Preparedness involves caring for both your users and staff as well as your facility and your collection. Preparedness means doing your best to prevent any disasters from occurring, knowing how to respond to disasters when they occur, and working together to successfully recover from a disaster.

The first step to being prepared is to create a team of staff members who will aid in prevention, response, and recovery during an emergency or disaster. This team will be known as the disaster team. Each member of the team will have different roles and responsibilities, which will be discussed in depth in this chapter.

After organizing your disaster team, you and the team will work together to create a disaster plan. This chapter concludes with developing this plan so that it will contain everything you need to successfully combat a disaster.

1

ORGANIZE A DISASTER TEAM

The disaster team should consist of a team leader and six coordinators. If you have sufficient staff, each coordinator should have at least one or two assistants. You may also consider asking coworkers outside the library for assistance if your staff is insufficient. For instance, if your library is a branch of a larger library system, you may be able to coordinate with another library and offer each other mutual assistance. Or if your library is on a college campus, consider who might be able to help you fill out your disaster team. Another option may be recruiting volunteers, though you should always check with your administration and get approval before doing so. Each coordinator should have an alternative in the event that person is not available. All assistants should report to their respective coordinators, and all coordinators should report to the disaster team leader.

Disaster Team Leader

The job of the disaster team leader is to oversee and manage the coordinators and act as a mediator should conflicts arise. The team leader will be responsible for evaluating all emergencies and declaring when the disaster plan will go into effect. During an evacuation, the team leader will be responsible for assigning the rest of the team members an area to evacuate. The team leader will also have the ability to authorize the purchase of necessary supplies and equipment as well as any emergency expenditures that are needed such as the hiring of a conservator or a mold removal service.

In choosing the disaster team leader, you need to ensure that this person is someone who is comfortable taking charge, making decisions, and managing a group of people. While the disaster team leader can seek the advice of the other members of the team, he or she will ultimately be responsible for the final decision of what actions to take.

Risk Assessment Coordinator

Because there are so many types of disasters or emergencies that can befall us, it would be impossible to be prepared for all of them; there simply are not enough hours in the day. The best thing that can be done is to undertake a risk assessment for the institution. The risk assessment coordinator must assess the risks most likely to occur at your library and should work with the team to develop procedures to eliminate or reduce the impact of those risks should they arise. Time is limited, and your focus should be on disasters and emergencies that the library is more likely to experience than not. In other words, you do not want the disaster team focusing on hurricane prevention response and recovery if you are located in Kansas. Instead you could be focusing on tornado prevention, response, and recovery, as this situation is far more likely to occur than a hurricane. The risk assessment coordinator will be responsible for day-to-day inspections of the building and the collections, evaluating the probability of occurrence for all types of disasters, and reevaluating those probabilities after a disaster or emergency occurs. In other words, the initial risk assessment for the occurrence of a hurricane might have been set as low risk, but if, for example, the library is hit by two hurricanes in two years, the risk assessment coordinator would be wise to change the risk level to high.

Operations Coordinator

The job of the operations coordinator is to oversee the overall operations of disaster planning and to ensure that all costs and losses are accurately tracked and documented. This means that the operations coordinator will mainly be in charge of procuring and replenishing salvage supplies and equipment, working with the team leader to authorize any emergency expenditures that may occur during a disaster, contacting the institution's insurance agent, and contacting any local, state, or federal authorities for any eligible financial assistance. If additional team members need to be recruited from outside your library staff, it is the operations coordinator who will take on this task.

During a disaster, the operations coordinator should inform the salvage coordinator of any procedures that must be followed for successful insurance claims. The operations coordinator will also help the salvage coordinator locate the needed supplies and help assemble them in the salvage area. The operations coordinator will regularly check in with the salvage coordinator to see if any additional supplies may be needed. He or she will also reach out to any emergency service vendors, if needed.

Communications Coordinator

The job of the communications coordinator involves communicating with the staff, emergency responders, and the press and media. Everyday tasks involve notifying the disaster team of any changes or updates in the disaster plan and communicating to the team the date and time of upcoming disaster tabletop exercises or practice drills.

During a disaster or emergency, the communications coordinator must set up a communications center with a computer; scanner; fax machine; phone; and contact list of press, media, board members, and anyone else who should be made aware of the emergency at hand. If the disaster is affecting more than just your library (e.g., hurricanes and flooding), the communications coordinator should stay informed of the situation and relay this information to the team leader and other coordinators. The person chosen for this role should be comfortable speaking in public and someone who can think on his or her feet.

Health and Safety Coordinator

The job of the health and safety coordinator is to prioritize the health and safety of staff and patrons as well as the safety of the facilities and the collection. He or she should be trained to be familiar with basic health and safety procedures. This coordinator needs to be familiar with emergency exits in order to efficiently evacuate staff and patrons from the building.

When it comes to the health and safety of the building and collection, the health and safety coordinator should understand how to detect a mold or pest infestation. This coordinator should have the contact information of a mycologist to identify toxic or dangerous mold and he or she should be well versed in integrated pest management (see Chapter 3, "Emergency Procedures: Prevention, Response, and Recovery"). Ensuring the building and collections are safe from theft is another responsibility of the health and safety coordinator. Make sure that there are logs for anyone entering or exiting the building to sign in and out, and check with the documentation coordinator that all photos, videos, and any additional documentation are complete before shutting down each day.

After a disaster or if evacuation has occurred, then the health and safety coordinator should make certain that no one enters the library until he or she has been given the okay by a building inspector, structural engineer, or a similarly qualified authority. When the salvage coordinator and helpers enter the facility, be sure that there is a nearby rest station for them to take breaks. Place signs around the area or verbally remind everyone in the salvage group to change out of oversoiled gloves on a regular basis or to wash their hands frequently if they choose not to wear gloves. It is the health and safety coordinator's role to ensure that everyone is wearing appropriate clothing and the necessary protective gear.

Documentation Coordinator

The job of the documentation coordinator is to document a disaster through photographs, video recordings, and condition reports. This coordinator will work closely with the salvage coordinator to properly document the damage caused by the disaster. The documentation coordinator should have at least two assistants: one to photograph or record the damage and another to take written notes. This coordinator should use the floor plans to indicate any structural damage, and as the salvage coordinator moves items in the collection to a salvage area, the documentation coordinator should make sure that each item is cataloged and its temporary location is listed (see the salvage relocation form example at the end of Chapter 5). If the documentation coordinator notices any dangerous structural issues, he or she should inform the health and safety coordinator, who in turn should have the area blocked off. The documentation coordinator should have an eye for detail and understands how important it is to keep records accurate.

Salvage Coordinator

This job involves understanding how to salvage various items in the library's collection. The person chosen for this job should have preservation and/or conservation experience. Because of the complicated process, the salvage coordinator should have at least two assistants. This coordinator will identify and attempt to protect or salvage the library's collection based on the salvage priority list that the disaster team has already created. The salvage coordinator should be able to know when an item is not salvageable and when a conservator needs to be called in for specialized assistance. The salvage coordinator will also need to work with the operations coordinator to arrange for any additional equipment and supplies needed during the salvage process. Anyone with allergies, respiratory problems, or compromised immune systems should not be chosen for this position.

WRITING A DISASTER PLAN

Now that you have your team members assigned, it is time to write a disaster plan. Institutions that have a disaster plan are far more likely to have less damage and resume operations sooner than those institutions with no disaster plan or an inadequate one. Your plan will be the go-to guide for best practices and procedures before, during, and after a disaster. It is important to remember that creating and enacting the plan is all about the team and teamwork; everyone needs to be involved and be able to work together. To help you start from scratch, this section will break down the creation of a disaster plan page by page.

Your disaster preparedness plan should begin with a table of contents. This will make it easier for anyone looking though the plan to figure out where to find relevant information. Your plan should have the following information:

- Disaster Team Contact Info
- Phone Tree
- Floor Plan
- Emergency Systems Locations List
- Salvage Priority List
- Emergency Services List
- Emergency Supplies Inventory
- Prevention, Response, and Recovery Procedures

- Communication Procedures
- Salvage Procedures
- Staff Training: Exercises and Drills
- Technology Tools

Disaster Team Contact Info

Under the Disaster Team Contact Info section, you should have the full name, e-mail address, work and cell phone or home number of each person on your disaster team in addition to what role they will play in the disaster team. Disasters can occur at any time of day, so you need a number to contact team members whether they are in the office or at home. A cell phone number is also good to have in case a disaster occurs while someone is out to lunch or en route to work. Ideally, you will contact human resources (HR) for all necessary information. HR is the best way to gather contact information because they will have the most up-to-date contact information for everyone.

Phone Tree

A phone tree is a communication tool that will allow you to notify particular individuals of an emergency or disaster and help you coordinate a response and recovery approach to the incident. Phone trees are beneficial in distributing time-sensitive information quickly, and they are a great way to communicate because no single person is responsible for calling everyone in the tree, so there is no burden on one individual. The phone tree will include all members of the disaster team as well as any other relevant persons. Once you know who will be included in the phone tree, you will need to decide on the calling sequence. The way the phone tree works is each person on the phone tree will contact the next person on the list and so on until everyone has been contacted. If the next person on the list cannot be reached, leave a message and continue with the next level of the phone tree so that the chain does not break. The last person on the list should confirm the completion of the phone tree by calling the phone tree initiator.

The person chosen to initiate the phone tree should be someone very reliable, as his or her execution (or lack thereof) of this communication tool will have a huge part in determining the success of response and recovery efforts. Ideally, the disaster team leader should be the phone tree initiator, but someone else (e.g., the communications coordinator) can be chosen if necessary. For the phone tree to be effective, limit the number of people each person must call, and keep the message short and concise. Only the facts should be given, and each caller should avoid hearsay. Confidentiality should be stressed. Update the phone tree at least quarterly to ensure the accuracy of the phone numbers and inclusion of all staff, and do a practice run of your phone tree at least once a year to make sure it is effective. Record the start and end time of the phone tree exercise to figure out how long it takes. Use this practice run to make any necessary improvements to the phone tree like correcting or updating staff's contact information. Document the practice run to compare it to future practice runs.

Floor Plan

Having a floor plan included in your disaster plan is important for team members and first responders to understand the layout in relation to the disaster and to locate important items. Your floor plan should include the locations of all exits, windows, stairways, elevators, first-aid kits, water detectors, smoke detectors, fire extinguishers, and utility shutoffs. The location of the items on your salvage priority list can be included on the floor plan as well to allow for faster retrieval. When creating the floor plan, try to use different colors to identify items easier. For those who find it hard to read floor plans, you can also create an "Emergency Systems" list where you list out each emergency system and its location.

Salvage Priority List

In this section, you will include a list of items that are to be prioritized for salvage in the case of an emergency or disaster. This list will help recovery efforts to be as efficient as possible. The team should sit down and create this list. Include any relevant people who are not on the disaster team in this discussion as well. Following are some guidelines in helping you decide what to salvage. Ideally, you would use these guidelines on an item level, but you may also use them on a collection level if necessary.

Value: Does the item have great historical value to your library?

Demand: Is this item in high demand? Do users regularly request this item?

Condition of Item: Is this item very fragile and likely to be destroyed completely in a disaster if not tended to immediately?

Availability: Is this item widely available? How easy would it be to replace the item?

Emergency Services List

During a disaster, you may find yourself in need of an emergency service. It is best to create a list of emergency services and make contact with them before a disaster occurs. Establishing relationships with emergency services before you need them allows you to make sure you properly understand the service(s) they provide. If a disaster strikes the whole community, there will be lots of people trying to acquire emergency services; already having a relationship with a particular service may give your institution an edge. Following is a list of the most common types of emergency services a library may need:

First Responders. Having the contact information of the local police and fire rescue services is extremely important because they will most likely be the first people you will call in a major disaster or emergency. Consider asking the police and fire services if they could provide a general safety demo to your staff on a yearly basis.

Security. You will want the contact information of whoever does the security for your library. They may need to be contacted in the event of a disaster or emergency. If your security is contracted out, make sure to have the security company's information as well.

The Insurance Company. Your library's insurance provider should be listed in the emergency services section. This will be one of the first and most important calls made after a disaster or emergency. Be sure to include information on how to file a claim and have a copy of the policy located with the disaster preparedness plan. If there is a particular agent that you deal with, include his or her name and contact information in the list.

Conservator and/or Preservation Specialist. If your collections experience major damage, your library may need to reach out to a conservator or preservation specialist who can help the salvage coordinator successfully salvage your items. Make sure that the conservator or preservation specialist has experience caring for the type of objects in your collection. Ensure that this person handles disaster recovery and is available on short notice. Have a backup conservator or preservation specialist in case your first choice is unavailable when disaster strikes.

Mold Removal Services. If you find yourself with a mold outbreak, you will want to contact a mold removal services vendor to help rid your library and collections of mold. Choose a vendor that has experience dealing with libraries. Consider also having the contact information of a mycologist to help you determine if you have toxic or dangerous mold in your library.

Emergency Supplies Inventory

To create your list, begin by going to Chapter 5 on salvaging procedures to look at the recovery and salvage procedures for disasters and emergencies that are the highest risk to your institution. Use those guidelines to create an emergency supplies list. Your list should detail what each item is, the quantity you have of each item, and the location of each item. You can arrange the list in alphabetical order, or you can arrange the list by category (cleaning, packing, safety, etc.). Your emergency supplies should be separate from everyday supplies. Staff should be informed not to use emergency supplies for everyday use. The operations coordinator should regularly do an inventory check of the emergency supplies to make sure the inventory matches what is in stock.

Emergency Procedures

This section provides the types of emergency procedures for emergencies or disasters that are a risk to your institution. These emergency procedures will list out clear instructions on what to do to prevent, prepare, and respond to each type of incident. Use the guidelines in Chapter 3 and the emergency procedures template provided at the end of this chapter to create customized emergency procedures for your institution's disaster plan. These include communication, and salvage procedures, staff training, and preferred technology tools.

Communication Procedures

This section of your plan will have all the information needed for the communications coordinator to do his or her job. This includes guidelines on how to develop a disaster communications plan, how to communicate during a disaster, and how to work with the press and media before and after a disaster. Effective communication is a key component to successfully responding and recovering from a disaster. See Chapter 4, "Communication Procedures," for more information.

Salvage Procedures

This section will contain the proper salvage procedures for the most commonly occurring damages such as water-related damage, fire-related damage, and mold-related damage. Successful salvaging usually happens within the first 48 hours of a disaster, and in order to act swiftly, you will need the proper salvaging procedures readily available. See Chapter 5, "Salvage Procedures," for more information.

Staff Training: Drills and Exercises

A huge part of being prepared for a disaster or emergency is regular staff training. This comes in the form of various practice drills and exercises. One of the main reasons disaster plans fail is when a plan is not exercised regularly. (See Figure 1.1.) Place the drills and exercises that pertain to the disasters most likely to occur in your institution in this section. See Chapter 6, "Staff Training: Exercises and Drills," for more information.

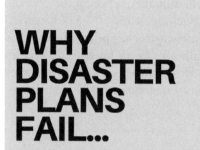

WHY DISASTER PLANS FAIL...

Plan is not exercised.

plans do not work if they remain on a shelf collecting dust. People are what make plans work, by being familiar with their contents.

Plan is outdated.

though time consuming, the disaster preparedness plan is a living document that needs to be reviewed, revised, and updated on a quarterly basis throughout the year.

Figure 1.1   Why Disaster Plans Fail

Technology Tools

You may be able to use a variety of technological tools and applications that can enhance your disaster preparedness plan. In this section, you should list the tools and apps that your disaster team will use. It is important to remind your team that these tech tools and apps are not to be used in place of a disaster preparedness plan, but rather to complement the plan. See Chapter 7, "Technology Tools," for more information.

DISTRIBUTING THE DISASTER PLAN

After the disaster plan is completed, it will need to be distributed. You should have multiple copies of the disaster plan in both physical and digital formats, and they should be in multiple locations.

Physical Copies

The disaster plan should be printed out and placed in a binder to create a disaster plan manual. The binder should be in a bright color like red so that it is easily noticeable. Because you never know when and where a disaster will strike, you should have multiple physical copies of the disaster plan. Have one physical copy for each floor of the library; having only one copy in the entire building or multiple copies on only one floor means staff on floors without the disaster plan will be at a disadvantage since it will take them longer to acquire the plan. In moments like these when every minute counts, there should be no extra obstacles to overcome. A physical copy on each floor of the library means quick access to response and salvage guidelines and increases the chances of successfully recovering from a disaster. Have at least one physical copy off-site (staff members can store a copy in their homes or vehicles). If a disaster occurs outside your hours of operation and the entire library has been blocked from entering because of safety issues, having an off-site copy of your disaster plan means having access to floor plans, salvage priority lists, and emergency service contacts. Handing over the floor plan to first responders may help them do their job quicker, and they may be able to prevent a minor disaster from turning into a major disaster.

Digital Copies

The disaster plan should also be available as a digital copy. If a team member cannot gain access to a physical copy of a disaster plan for whatever reason, having a digital copy available can be very helpful.

There are various places to keep a digital copy of your disaster plan. The first place institutions think of putting their disaster plan up is on their website. It is easy for staff to remember the web address in an emergency, and it is accessible by anyone with an Internet connection. If you choose to go this route, it is recommended that the disaster plan webpage be password-protected. Many portions of a customized disaster plans should not be available to the general public. For example, the floor plan in particular is full of highly sensitive information. Someone wishing to commit arson or plant a bomb or an active shooter can use your floor plan to gain knowledge they might not ordinarily have. Your floor plan will also have the location of the most valuable items in your collection; the purpose for this is for disaster team members to quickly locate these items to save them from extensive damage. But when your floor plan is available to the general public, a thief might use this information to steal your valuable items. This is why it is recommended that any highly sensitive information in the disaster plan be on webpages that require a password for access. If your library chooses to place your disaster plan on a flash drive or a CD, make sure that all highly sensitive documents (floor plan, evacuation procedures, etc.) are password-protected.

This chapter has provided an introduction to disaster planning including building a disaster team and described the members and their roles and responsibilities. It also described what is needed in building a disaster plan. The next chapter will describe common disasters and emergencies to help in the risk assessment portion of your disaster plan.

Day-to-Day Tasks	Emergency Response Tasks
• Regularly touch base with the disaster team coordinators to see if you can be of any help with their day-to-day tasks.	• Assign an evacuation area for staff and patrons to go to.
	• Check in with all disaster team coordinators throughout and after the emergency.
• Organize disaster team tabletop exercises and practice drills.	
	• Authorize the purchase of necessary supplies and equipment as well as any emergency expenditures that are needed.
• Evaluate situations in the library as they arise and enact the disaster plan if necessary.	
	• Act as a mediator should conflicts arise.

Figure 1.2   Team Leader Tasks

Day-to-Day Tasks	Emergency Response Tasks
• Assess the risks most likely to occur at your library and work with the team to develop procedures to eliminate or reduce the impact of those risks.	• Work with the health and safety coordinator to assess risk.
• Organize regular inspections of the building and the collection.	• Reevaluate the likelihood of each risk after every disaster.
• Participate in disaster team tabletop exercises and practice drills.	

Figure 1.3 Risk Assessment Coordinator Tasks

Day-to-Day Tasks	Emergency Response Tasks
• Procure and replenish salvage supplies and equipment.	• Contact the library's insurance agent, and contact any local, state, or federal authorities for financial assistance, if eligible.
• Recruit additional members for the disaster team, if needed.	• Work with the disaster team leader to get authorization for the purchase of additional supplies and equipment as well as for any emergency expenditures that are needed.
• Keep track of the library's insurance policy (i.e., what it covers, when it needs to be renewed, etc.)	
• Participate in disaster team tabletop exercises and practice drills.	• Help the salvage coordinator locate the needed supplies and help assemble them in the salvage area.
	• Regularly check in with the salvage coordinator to see if any additional supplies may be needed.
	• Reach out to any emergency service vendors, if needed.

Figure 1.4   Operations Coordinator Tasks

Day-to-Day Tasks	Emergency Response Tasks
• Notify the disaster team members of any changes or updates in the disaster plan.	• Set up a communications center with a computer, scanner, fax machine, phone, and contact list of press, media, and board members.
• Work with the risk assessment coordinator to understand what disasters your institution is at highest risk for.	• Work with the disaster team leader to get authorization for the purchase of additional supplies and equipment as well as for any emergency expenditures that are needed.
• Put together an effective communications plan to be used during a disaster.	• Help the salvage coordinator locate the needed supplies and help assemble them in the salvage area.
• Communicate to the team the date and time of upcoming disaster tabletop exercises or practice drills.	• Regularly check in with the salvage coordinator to see if any additional supplies may be needed.
• Participate in disaster team tabletop exercises and practice drills.	• Reach out to any emergency service vendors, if needed.
• Participate in mock press conferences.	

Figure 1.5   Communications Coordinator Tasks

Day-to-Day Tasks	Emergency Response Tasks
• Keep up to date with basic health and safety procedures.	• Check with emergency responders or other qualified authority for approval before reentering the building.
• Learn how to detect a mold or pest infestation.	• Ensure that everyone entering the building is wearing appropriate clothing and necessary protective gear.
• Be well-versed in integrated pest management policies.	• Create a nearby rest station with seats and water for anyone participating in the salvage process.
• Participate in disaster team tabletop exercises and practice drills.	• Check with the documentation coordinator that all photos, videos, and any additional documentation are complete before shutting down each day.

Figure 1.6 Health and Safety Coordinator Tasks

Day-to-Day Tasks	Emergency Response Tasks
• Put together the disaster plan manual. • Participate in disaster team tabletop exercises and practice drills. • Document the results of all tabletop exercises and practice drills.	• Check with the health and safety coordinator before reentering the library. • Work closely with the salvage coordinator to properly document the damage caused by the disaster. • Make sure that each item is cataloged and its temporary location is listed. • If there are any dangerous structural issues, inform the health and safety coordinator who in turn should have the area blocked off. • Confirm with the health and safety coordinator that all photos, videos, and any additional documentation are complete before shutting down each day.

Figure 1.7 Documentation Coordinator Tasks

Day-to-Day Tasks	Emergency Response Tasks
• Learn salvage techniques that pertain to the most common items in the collection.	• Check with the health and safety coordinator before attempting any salvage procedures.
• Practice salvage techniques at least one to two times a year.	• Locate items on salvage priority list in the library.
• Work with the operations coordinator in selecting emergency supplies.	• Salvage collection from disaster-related damage.
	• Work with the documentation coordinator to document the damage to the collection.
• Participate in disaster team tabletop exercises and practice drills.	• Work with the operations coordinator to replenish supplies during salvage procedures.
	• Work with the operations coordinator to find a conservator if necessary.

Figure 1.8   Salvage Coordinator Tasks

[Your Library's Name] Disaster Plan

Table of Contents

Page #

Figure 1.9   Table of Contents Template

Name	E-mail Address	Phone Number	Team Role	Last Updated
Jane Doe	janedoe@library.org	Work: 555-1234 ext. 10 Home: 555-3390 Cell: 555-4545	Team Leader	10/01/17
John Smith	johnsmith@library.org	Work: 555-1234 ext. 12 Home: N/A Cell: 555-3999	Salvage Coordinator	10/01/17
Jennifer Adams	jadams@library.org	Work: 555-1234 ext. 15 Home: 555-8890 Cell: 555-4470	Health and Safety Coordinator	12/01/17

Jennifer got a new cell phone number in December. Contact info was updated to reflect new number.

Figure 1.10   Contact Info Example

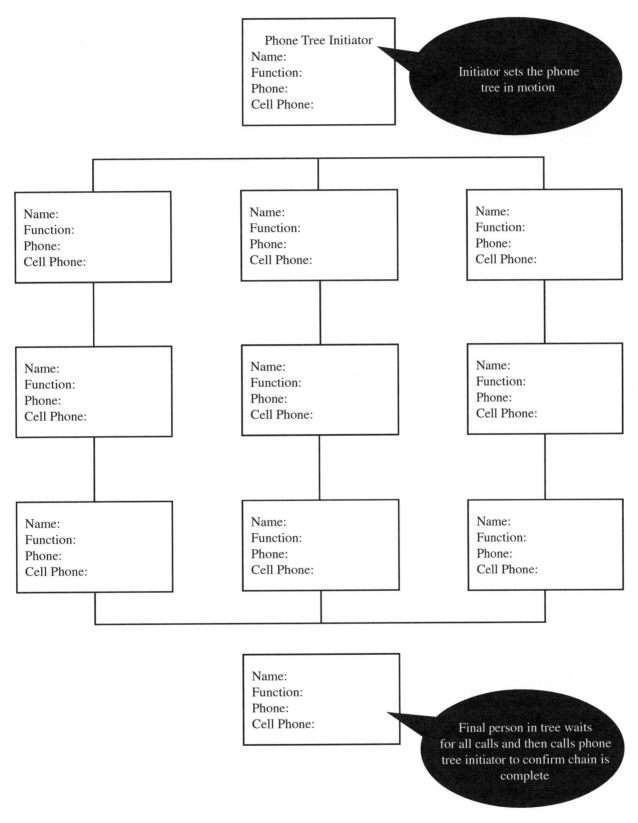

Figure 1.11 Phone Tree Template

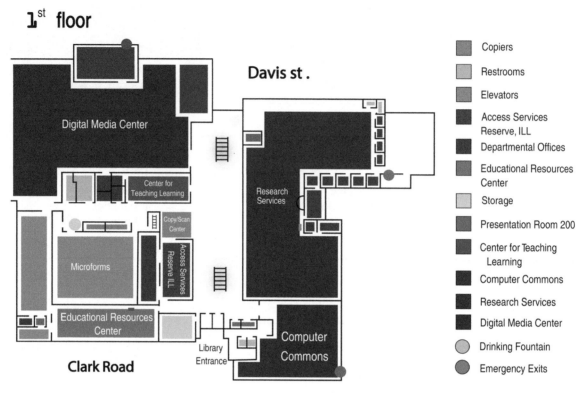

Figure 1.12 Floor Plan Example

Use this template to create a customized Emergency Systems Location List

Emergency System		Location
Main Utilities	Main water shutoff valve(s)	
	Sprinkler shutoff valve(s)	
	Main electrical disconnects	
	Main gas shutoffs	
	Heating and cooling system controls	
Fire Suppression Systems	Sprinklers	
Fire Extinguishers	Fire extinguisher #1	
	Fire extinguisher #2	
Smoke Detectors	Smoke detector #1	
	Smoke detector #2	
Keys	Master keys	
	Special keys	
Public Address System		

Figure 1.13 Locations of Emergency Systems Template

In order of priority, list the library and archive materials that should be salvaged first. When completing the form, consider what you would salvage if you had only a few hours to effect the recovery. Describe the collection briefly and give the location by indicating the building, floor, room number, and so on. Describe the type of material (books, manuscripts, photographs, graphics) and the quantity.

Catalog/Call Number	Collection/Item	Location	Type of Material	Quantity

Figure 1.14 Salvage Priorities List Form

	[Insert Service Provider Here]	ABC Mold Removal Services	Magnolia Conservators
Contact Person	If you have a contact person at the company, enter his or her name here.	Jason Chen	Elizabeth Rodriguez
Phone Number	1. Business hours phone number 2. After hours phone number	1. 555-4545 2. 555-9990	1. 555-1212 2. 555-1212
Fax Number	Enter the service provider's fax number here.	1. 555-4546	1. 555-1213
E-mail Address	1. General e-mail address 2. Contact person's e-mail address	1. info@abcmold.com 2. jasonc@abcmold.com	1. info@ magnoliaconservators .com 2. erodriguez@magnolia conservators.com
Physical Address	Enter the physical address and/or the mailing address here.	3203 Carlisle St Boston, MA 02116	1234 Magnolia Lane Brooklyn, NY 11215
Notes	Add any notes you might need here.	N/A	Specializes in rare books.

Figure 1.15   Emergency Services Form Example

Item	Quantity	Location
CLIP BOARD	2	Bin #1, 1st Floor Storage Closet
FIRST-AID KIT	1	Bin #2, 1st Floor Storage Closet
HEPA VACUUM	1	2nd Floor Storage Closet
NITRILE GLOVES	2 boxes	Bin #2, 1st Floor Storage Closet
PAPER (BLANK, 8.5" × 11")	2 packages of 200 sheets	Bin #1, 1st Floor Storage Closet
PAPER (COLLEGE RULED, 8.5" × 11")	2 packages of 250 sheets	Bin #1, 1st Floor Storage Closet
PAPER TOWELS	24	Bin #3, 1st Floor Storage Closet
PENCIL SHARPENER (MANUAL)	2	Bin #1, 1st Floor Storage Closet
PENCILS	24	Bin #1, 1st Floor Storage Closet
SAFETY GOGGLES	2	Bin #2, 1st Floor Storage Closet
SPONGES (PVA)	5	Bin #2, 1st Floor Storage Closet

Figure 1.16   Emergency Supplies Inventory Example

Prevention, Response, and Recovery Procedures Template

Create a procedure form for each disaster considered a risk to your library. Use the guidelines in Chapter 3, "Emergency Procedures" to guide you through this template. Do not forget to customize the guidelines for your institution.

What can we do to prevent [Insert Disaster/Emergency Here]?

What can we do to prepare for [Insert Disaster/Emergency Here]?

How do we respond to [Insert Disaster/Emergency Here]?

Figure 1.17

CHAPTER 2

Common Disasters and Emergencies

In order to successfully prepare for a disaster, you will need to conduct a risk assessment specific to your library. This is done by identifying the disasters and emergencies that are considered high risk to your institution. This chapter will break down the most commonly occurring disasters and emergencies and help you decide if your library is at risk.

WATER-RELATED DISASTERS

Of all the disasters a library might experience, water-related disasters are the most common, and they cause the most damage to a library's collections. Institutions can experience water-related damages from a variety of sources, such as floods, which cause the most damage, structural-related, or a combination of the two.

Floods

Floods can be described as an overflow of water onto normally dry land. Floods can happen for a variety of reasons including heavy rains, snow that melts too fast, and dams or levees that break. Flooding may happen with only a few inches of water, or it may cover a building up to the rooftop. They can occur quickly or over a long period and may last for days, weeks, or longer. Floods are the most common and prevalent of all weather-related natural disasters.[1]

The Dangers of Floods

Flood water in urban areas can carry dangerous bacteria that could potentially cause diseases. Flood water in rural areas can be contaminated with agricultural chemicals and animal waste. Flood water can also contain sharp and dangerous objects that pose potential risks, since they are hidden from sight under water that can be muddy or murky. Flash floods can be particularly dangerous. A flash flood is a sudden intense flooding that can take anywhere from minutes to hours to develop. Flash floods can be caused by a number of things but is most often due to extremely heavy rainfall from thunderstorms.

Flood Warning versus Flood Watch

The National Weather Service provides four different types of flood-related alerts: flood watch, flood warning, flash flood warning, and flood advisory. The first, flood watch alert, is issued when conditions are favorable for flooding. This does not mean flooding will occur, but it means that flooding is possible. A flood warning alert is issued when flooding is imminent or already occurring. A flash flood warning is issued when flash flooding is imminent or already occurring. It is given for a flood advisory.

A flood advisory is a warning that is issued when flooding is expected or already occurring but the flooding is not considered a significant threat to life or property. This type of alert is used for nuisance flooding problems, such as flooding in low-lying areas and areas of poor drainage, as well as minor flooding of streets and roadways.[2]

Is My Institution at Risk?

Flooding can occur at any time of the year, and it is a threat experienced anywhere in the world that receives rain. In the United States, floods kill more people each year than tornadoes or hurricanes. When it comes to flash floods, certain locations are considered at high risk, including densely populated areas and areas near rivers and mountainous regions.

Densely populated areas are at high risk for flash flooding because most urban areas have a high concentration of paved-over areas for sidewalks, roads, and highways, so there is less space for the rain water to be absorbed by the ground. This runoff increases the likelihood of a flash flood. Levees are often built along rivers to prevent water from flooding the surrounding land, and because levees can fail, this makes areas near rivers high risk as well. Finally, mountains and steep hills produce rapid runoff, which causes streams to rise quickly because rocks and clay soils do not allow much water to infiltrate the ground.[3]

Real-Life Examples of Floods

Example #1: On July 26, 2017, in Salt Lake City, Utah, heavy rain flooded the Sprague Branch of the Salt Lake City Public Library building overnight. The rushing water went down the library's emergency stairwell, breaking windows and doors and flooding the rooms in the basement. By the time the library maintenance crew arrived in the morning, the basement was under 5 feet of water, and everything from children's books to computers to the basement walls were damaged by the water. The library took several months to recover and reopen. The estimated damage to the library was around $1.5 million to $2 million. The library did not have flood insurance because the price was cost-prohibitive, so most of the money had to come from the library system's budget.[4]

Example #2: On November 15, 2017, one of the children's rooms in the historic Jefferson Carnegie Library in Jefferson, Texas, sustained extensive flooding damage. It is not known what exactly caused the water to leak into the library, but investigators think that rain may have built up in the gutters and that water came down through the chimney and leaked through the walls on the first floor.[5] Approximately 430 books were lost.

Example #3: Heavy rainfall caused the basement of the Grace A. Dow Memorial Library in Midland, Michigan, to be flooded in June 2017. As water began to enter the building through a drain, the sump pumps could not keep up with the amount of water that was coming into the basement. Not only did they lose the entire collection that was housed in the basement, but they also lost furniture, carpeting, and walls that were damaged by the flooding. The damage to the collection and building was estimated at $1.5 million.[6] While the library had insurance, it was not able to cover the entire cost of the restoration and cleanup. The library had to turn to grants and donations to make up the difference.

Structural Damage

Your library may experience water damage due to structural damage. The most common types of structural damage are leaking roofs and leaking pipes.

The Dangers of Structural Damage

If your electrical wiring is present in the ceiling, a leaky roof could pose a fire threat from shorted wires. Leaking roofs or pipes can also cause puddles, which can cause slip and fall accidents. In the long term, one of the most serious consequences of a leaking roof is mold growth.

Is My Institution at Risk?

All institutions are at risk of a leaking roof or pipes, so it is important to regularly inspect the roof and pipes. If damage is found, it is important to document this and have it repaired as soon as possible. If your insurance company suspects you were aware of a leak and did nothing to fix the problem, you may not be covered when a disaster strikes.

Real-Life Examples of Structural Damage

Example #1: A July 2017 windstorm in Phoenix, Arizona, damaged the Burton Barr Central Library's roof and caused the sprinkler system to confuse dust with smoke. This sent water spewing through the library's corroded pipes, which burst under the pressure, flooding every corner of the historic building. About 50 to 60 gallons-a-minute of water started flowing through the building. To put that in context, a fire hydrant typically sprays 90 gallons of water per minute.[7] At least two years earlier, major corrosion issues were brought to the attention of at least six employees, though none of them properly alerted supervisors. In addition, alarms that were set up to alert staff of leaks in the piping were shut off and ignored. The flooding from the corroded pipes cost the library approximately $10 million in repairs.[8] Due to the negligence, three city employees were terminated, two were demoted, and one was suspended.

Example #2: In the spring of 2017, the Tustin Library in California's Orange County discovered a slow leak in its subfloor, and the library was immediately evacuated because of concerns about the electrical wiring that was also beneath the floor. The water did extensive damage to the wiring, and the main library remained closed for months while it awaited a damage assessment by the city's insurer. Fortunately, the library's 105,000 books were not damaged, but they remained in the building untouched for all those months until inspectors considered the structure safe for employees to reenter.[9]

Example #3: In February 2015, the Manchester City Library in New Hampshire lost thousands of books and eight computers when a main sprinkler pipe burst. For almost four hours, water poured from the burst pipe. By the time the water was shut off to the building, more than 5 feet of water filled the lower level of the building.[10] In this case, the cold weather was to blame; the low temperature caused the pipe to freeze. While a library custodian had reported it, the city's crew did not know where the valve was located, and because it was buried under the snow, this added to the difficulty in finding it. Unfortunately, the pipe burst before the situation could be remedied.

MOLD AND PESTS

Mold outbreaks and pest infestations are common disasters that are likely to occur in your library at one time or another. Mold is a general term for fungi that occur naturally in the environment. Mold grows through the spreading of its spores, which are always present in the air waiting for the right opportunity to germinate. Because mold grows on any organic material, including paper, adhesives, leather, dust, and dirt, mold spores are practically everywhere. Mold can be active or dormant.

Dangers of Mold

A mold outbreak is a very serious matter. Mold is dangerous to the health of employees and anyone coming into your institution, as well as the items in your collection.

Human Health Risks

Active mold can be the source of respiratory problems, skin and eye irritation, and infections in humans. These reactions may be the result of either short-term exposure to high concentrations of mold or long-term exposure to low concentrations. Whether the mold is active or dormant makes no difference; the degree of risk from exposure to mold is determined by a person's general health and preexisting sensitivity to mold as well as the concentration of the mold bloom. Staff members who have compromised immune systems or have known sensitivity to mold (e.g., allergy to penicillin) should not have contact with any materials containing mold.[11]

Collection Risks

Active mold will produce enzymes that can digest organic materials such as paper and book cloth, which will weaken or destroy them. Colorful blooms can also cause stains that cannot be removed. Active mold poses an immediate risk to your collections and should be addressed without delay.[12] Inactive mold, on the other hand, poses no immediate danger to your collections, except that it can be spread through handling and air currents and will readily bloom if propitious environmental conditions occur.

Libraries located in humid tropical regions will be most vulnerable, but there is still a risk of mold occurring anywhere in the world if the environmental conditions in your library are not satisfactory, especially during the warm weather months. Any library that is not regularly monitoring the temperature and relative humidity levels of its building is at risk of a mold outbreak.

Real-Life Examples of Mold

Example #1: In the fall of 2007, the University of Illinois at Urbana–Champaign's Rare Book and Manuscript Library suffered a mold outbreak due to high humidity levels in the library. It took the library staff eight months to establish and implement a proper plan of attack. They first tried to get the relative humidity down to recommended levels, and then they sought out the help of a mycologist to help understand the kind of mold they were dealing with. Once the mycologist determined that they did not have a toxic form of mold, the library conservators spent 60 hours on an item-level assessment of the collection. Through the assessment, they learned that the mold had spread throughout the collection but had fortunately not caused any irreparable damage. Only 5 percent of the library's 300,000 items had visible mold, but because mold was present near and in the heating, ventilation, and air-conditioning (HVAC) system, all the items had to be treated. Because so many items were affected, the library staff chose to outsource the mold cleanup. The cleanup was estimated to cost approximately $800,000.[13]

Example #2: On August 9, 2013, an outbreak of nontoxic mold was discovered on the fifth floor of the University of Maryland's McKeldin Library. The cause for the mold outbreak was high humidity levels throughout the summer. It was estimated that 10 to 20 percent of the floor's 200,000 books were contaminated by the mold, but because of the way mold propagates, all of the items had to be cleaned. Like in the case of the mold outbreak at the library at the University of Illinois Urbana–Champaign, the McKeldin Library chose to outsource the mold cleanup due to the large amount of items affected. The cost of the cleanup was estimated at $100,000.[14]

Example #3: In September 2015, the Boston Public Library had to close its Rare Book Department after mold was found on some materials in the collection. Though the library staff usually monitors the building's humidity and uses dehumidifiers to combat high humidity levels, the warm summer weather combined with the major renovations the library was undergoing at the time (making it harder to control temperature and relative humidity levels) are thought to be the culprits. The Boston Public Library also chose to outsource its mold cleanup, which they estimated to be approximately $250,000.[15]

PEST INFESTATION

Insects, rodents, and other pests feed on cellulose, adhesives, sizing, and other organic substances found in library collections. Common pests include roaches, book lice, silverfish, beetles, and rodents. Damage to your collection is caused not just by eating, but also by tunneling, nesting, and bodily secretions. Rats, mice, squirrels, birds, and other small animals can also cause significant damage to paper collections. Since some insects and pests are attracted to the tight, dark places that are plentiful in storage areas and since many collection materials are handled infrequently, these insects and other pests may cause significant damage before they are discovered.

The Dangers of Pest Infestation

The damage they cause to collections is irreversible. An estimated 6 million species of insects make up the majority of living creatures on Earth. More than 70 different species have been identified as enemies of paper. Pests also cause serious health risks to staff and patrons. Hantavirus pulmonary syndrome (HPS) is a deadly respiratory disease that humans can get when virus-containing particles from rodent urine, droppings, or saliva are stirred into the air. It can also be transmitted when hantavirus-infected particles or droplets come into contact with your nose, eyes, or mouth transferred from your hands. Cases of HPS have occurred in at least 30 of the continental 48 states. Untreated cases of HPS are almost always fatal, making this one of the most serious dangers faced when there is a pest infestation.

Is My Institution at Risk of a Pest Infestation?

Any institution that does not properly monitor temperature, relative humidity, and potential food sources is at high risk for a pest infestation. Areas that are naturally high in both temperature and humidity will be at highest risk for pest infestation. Any institution that does not practice integrated pest management (see Chapter 3: "Emergency Procedures: Prevention, Response, and Recovery") will also be at high risk.

Real-Life Examples of Pest Infestation

Example #1: In 2009, the Denver Public Library had a patron who lived in a building infested with bed bugs. He frequently borrowed many of the library's rare books and unfortunately ended up infecting 31 books with bed bugs. The pages of the books were stained so heavily by bed bug droppings that they had to be destroyed. The cost of the destroyed books was estimated at $12,000. The library also had to pay $6,000 in fumigation costs to eliminate the infestation.[16]

Example #2: In 2005, clothes moths were found in a display case at the Pitt Rivers Museum at Oxford University, and despite being treated straight away, the problem spread to other cases. Pest damage is a serious threat to collections because their damage is mostly irreversible. The Pitt Rivers Museum has an enormous costume collection that could easily be destroyed by quickly multiplying moths.[17]

Example #3: In 2013, the Museum of Islamic Art (MIA) in Doha, Qatar, had an historic swords exhibition entitled, "Steel and Gold." One of the items brought in for the exhibition was a depiction of an ancient sword, which was found to be chewed full of holes by pests. Fortunately, MIA's conservation lab was able to restore the object for the exhibition.[18]

MEDICAL EMERGENCIES

Medical emergencies that you may experience at the library will be varied; everything from minor falls to asthma attacks to heart attacks can and do occur. Medical emergencies may also occur after another disaster; it is not uncommon to deal with injuries due to earthquake, tornado, or hurricane damage, and there is also the chance of medical emergencies after an active shooter situation or a bomb detonation. Recently, some public libraries have also had to deal with patrons overdosing on drugs in the bathrooms or elsewhere on the premises.

Dangers Involved in Medical Emergencies

Any major medical emergency has the potential of being life-threatening, but cardiac arrest and drug overdose are two major medical emergencies. Each year, over 350,000 out-of-hospital cardiac arrests occur in the United States.[19] Cardiac arrest is an electrical malfunction in the heart that causes an irregular heartbeat and disrupts the flow of blood to the brain, lungs, and other organs. Death can follow within a matter of minutes unless a normal heart rhythm is restored. Immediate cardiopulmonary resuscitation (CPR) and the use of automatic external defibrillators (AEDs) can restore a heart's natural rhythm. From 2000 to 2015, more than half a million people died from drug overdoses, and more than 6 out of 10 of those overdoses involved an opioid.[20] A library staff trained in lifesaving techniques can help minimize the severity of a medical emergency.

Is My Institution at Risk of a Medical Emergency?

Because medical emergencies can happen to anyone anywhere, almost all libraries will be at risk for a medical emergency occurring on their premises. If your library has a high proportion of elderly patrons, your risk is high for a variety of medical emergencies occurring. If your community has been hit by the current opioid crisis, you should assess the risk of drug overdoses occurring at your institution as high. If your library is located in an Asthma Capital (like Detroit, Philadelphia, or Memphis), you should assess the risk of asthma attacks as high. As mentioned previously, medical emergencies may happen as a result of a natural disaster, so if your library is at high risk for natural disasters, you should consider yourself at high risk for medical emergencies as well.

Real-Life Examples of Medical Emergencies

Example #1: Opioid Crisis: In 2016, a staff member at the Humboldt County Library in California noticed a man who appeared to be sleeping at a table near the reference desk. Upon further inspection, the staff member could see that the man "had mucus coming out of his nose, and his breathing was kind of gurgly, and his lips were blue." She figured that he was having an overdose. One staff member called 911, while another injected the man with a dose of Narcan, a drug that reverses the effects of opiate overdose. When he didn't respond, the staff member followed protocol by giving him a second dose, at which point he appeared to be responsive. The paramedics arrived a short while later.[21]

Example #2: Cardiac Arrests: In 2011, the Federation of Friends of DC Public Library and Mended Hearts, Inc. jointly raised $35,000 to have AEDs installed in every DC Public Library. The Cheney Cardiovascular Institute donated the remaining costs for the AEDs as well as CPR training for nearly 100 library staff members as part of its ReStart DC program. These organizations worked hard to ensure that district residents in every ward have access to lifesaving heart equipment and CPR-trained staff when they visit a library.[22]

THEFT

While you may not think of theft as a disaster, the repercussions of theft of collection items can be disastrous to the library in many ways. The theft of books, CDs, DVDs, and other material from public libraries is a national problem, one that is thought to cost taxpayers millions of dollars a year. Library theft is not a recent problem by any stretch of the imagination; it is an ongoing issue that dates all the way back to antiquity.

The Dangers of Theft

Because there are many objects in libraries that are unique or rare, the theft of these valuable items from institutions is a serious problem for the preservation of recorded history. In addition, once these items are stolen and if they are placed on the black market, they are rarely returned back to the original owner. The Museum Security Network, a Dutch-based, not-for-profit organization whose focus is on combatting book theft, estimates that only 2 to 5 percent of stolen books are recovered.

Is My Institution at Risk of Theft?

Libraries that are at the highest risk for theft are rare book libraries and institutions that have a special collections department with rare and/or unique items. If you have a large collection of materials dealing with the occult, Satanism, witchcraft, or astrology, your risk for theft is high; a survey from the American Library Association found that books on these topics are the most stolen.[23] Libraries that do not properly vet their employees and volunteers are also at high risk; it is estimated that "inside jobs" account for upwards of 70 percent of all library theft in Europe and 80 percent in the United States.[24]

Real-Life Examples of Theft

Example #1: In February 2014, Russell Graves, a janitor in the Bangor Public Library, stole 75 Civil War–era photographs and 50 original World War I and World War II posters. He walked into collectibles dealer, Maritime International, attempting to sell the photographs and posters. What Graves did not know was that, by the time he brought them to the dealer, the owner of Maritime International had already seen the items at the library a few weeks earlier. Graves had often spent time in the special collections area, claiming he was cleaning, while in reality he was stealing historical artifacts and documents to sell for a profit. The items had an estimated value of $31,000, and Graves was later charged with a felony.

Example #2: Rebecca Streeter-Chen was the curator at the Rockland County Historical Society in April 2007, when she stole the institute's most-prized possession, a $60,000 Tanner Atlas. Thankfully, it was immediately recognized as missing, and the requisite warnings sent out. Because the item was quickly reported as stolen, Streeter-Chen was apprehended when she offered it for sale to a Philadelphia antiquarian map dealer only a few hours after the theft. She was sentenced to five years' probation and 24 weekends of community service.

Example #3: Daniel Lorello was an archivist at the New York State Library and a long-time thief; he specialized in stealing and selling low-value historical documents, allowing his thefts to go unnoticed for some time. Lorello targeted these items because he rightfully assumed these things would be neither missed nor recognized when put up for sale. Eventually his luck ran out when someone recognized one of the stolen items, and Lorello was reported to the authorities. In his confession to the police, he claimed to have stolen more than 400 items. Lorello pleaded guilty to grand larceny in 2008 and was sentenced to two to six years; however, he was granted early release on April 28, 2010.

Example #4: In 1986, Skeet Willingham was the head of Special Collections at the University of Georgia. He stole an eight-volume set of floral prints by 19th-century artist Pierre-Joseph Redoute worth $500,000. As the head of Special Collections, Willingham had access to the library's catalog, and he used this access to scrub the catalog clean of the existence of the floral prints. His thinking was somewhere along the lines of "I can't be found stealing something that doesn't exist." What Willingham didn't know, however, was that a photocopy of the library's catalog card had been made for, and stored at, the university's science library as a cross-reference. Willingham was sentenced to 15 years in prison and ordered to pay the state Board of Regents $45,000 for stealing rare and valuable library material.

Example #5: Over many years, Library Director of the Girolamini Library in Naples, Marino Massimo De Caro, rearranged books and destroyed catalog cards to make it difficult to track perhaps as many as 3,000 items he stole from the collection. Because only half of the approximately 170,000 books in the collection were ever cataloged, no one is sure exactly how many books were stolen. De Caro was found guilty of embezzlement and sentenced to seven years' imprisonment and lifetime exclusion from public office.

FIRE-RELATED DISASTERS

If a fire takes your collection, it is often gone. If the fire does not destroy your collection, then the water from the fire hoses wielded by the fireman trying to put out the fire will likely damage or destroy them. The most common causes of fire-related damage in libraries are due to electrical issues, arson, or wildfires. On average, more than 100,000 wildfires clear 4 to 5 million acres of land in the United States every year. Four out of five wildfires are started by humans.[25] Of all the discussed disasters, your collection is least likely to survive a fire. The good news is that most fires are preventable.

Dangers of Fire-Related Disasters

One reason that fires are so dangerous is that they move fast. It takes mere seconds for a fire to double in size and less than a minute to rage out of control and fill the area with heat and smoke. The heat and smoke given off from a fire can be deadly; most people who die in fires die from a combination of toxic gases, thick black smoke, and lack of oxygen.[26]

Wildfire Warnings

When it comes to wildfire disasters, the National Weather Service issues three types of warnings. A Fire Weather Watch may be issued when the potential for severe fire weather is expected to develop within the next 12 to 48 hours. A Red Flag Warning may be issued for severe fire weather events less than 12 hours away from occurring. While many assume that a Red Flag Warning will be preceded by a Fire Weather Watch, this is not always the case. Extreme fire behavior occurs when a wildfire is raging out of control. These types of fires can be hard to predict because they behave erratically and sometimes dangerously. Extreme fire behavior is at hand if the fire has at least one of the following criteria:

- Moving fast: High rate of spread
- Prolific crowning and/or spotting
- Presence of fire whirls
- Strong convection column[27]

Is My Institution at Risk of a Fire-Related Disaster?

Wildfires can happen anywhere, but they are most common in the forested areas of the United States and Canada, with wildfires also occurring in the vegetated areas of Australia and the Western Cape of South Africa. Wildfires are particularly widespread in the summer, fall, and winter, especially during dry periods with high winds.

Though arson can happen to any institution, libraries that have a high number of young patrons are at the highest risk, since most arsonists are young in age, with 40 percent of those arrested for arson under the age of 18. Libraries that are within schools are also at high risk, as schools are one of the main targets of arsonists. Since most arson fires occur at night, institutions with little to no security after working hours will also be considered high risk.

Libraries with overloaded electrical plug points and extension cables are considered high risk for electrical fires, since this can cause an unsafe rise in temperature. Faulty cable splices, damaged or frayed wires, or cut insulation can be an extreme fire hazard.

Real-Life Examples of Fire-Related Disasters

Example #1: On September 13, 2000, there was an electrical fire in the basement of Bush Memorial Library at Hamline University in St. Paul, Minnesota. Shortly before the library was to close, the fire was detected, and the library staff and students were quickly evacuated. The collection items in the basement had fire-related damage as well as water damage due to the firefighters' efforts to put out the fire. Because smoke circulated to all three upper floors through the ventilation system, it deposited a fine layer of soot on the entire collection of 277,000 items. The library's conservators hired a firm to take every single book and video out of the library and vacuum it by hand.[28]

Example #2: On Thanksgiving day in 2003, the Laurel Creek Elementary School in Fairfield, California, was set ablaze by an arsonist. The fire was started at approximately 11 P.M. when a planter outside the building was set on fire, and the flames crept through a window. The fire damaged a portion of the library's 11,000 books and destroyed 20 computers worth $25,000. The total damage from the arson was estimated to be $100,000.

Example #3: In October 2017, the Santa Rosa wildfires in California destroyed thousands of important papers belonging to the founders of Silicon Valley's first technology company, Hewlett-Packard. None of the items in the Hewlett-Packard archives that were destroyed had been digitized. The archive had been valued at nearly $2 million in 2005. The former Hewlett-Packard staff archivist believed the damage could have been preventable. The archivist noted that previous owners had stored the collections in vaults within permanent facilities, safeguarded by foam fire retardant. The current keepers of these records had them stored in two modular buildings.

ACTIVE SHOOTER

The United States Department of Homeland Security defines the active shooter as "an individual actively engaged in killing or attempting to kill people in a confined and populated area; in most cases, active shooters use firearms(s) and there is no pattern or method to their selection of victims."[29] Active shooters fall into four types of categories: The first type includes criminals who have no other connection with the location but enter to commit robbery or another crime. The second type is customers, clients, patients, students, or any others for whom an organization provides services. The third type is disgruntled present or former employees. The fourth type is individuals who do not work at the location but have a personal relationship with an employee.[30]

The Dangers of an Active Shooter Situation

Because active shooter situations are unpredictable and evolve quickly, they have the potential to be very dangerous. Most active shooter situations are often over within 10 to 15 minutes before law enforcement even has the chance to arrive. In these situations, there is usually no reasoning or bargaining that can be done with the perpetrator, as they usually enter this situation expecting to die.

Is My Institution at Risk of an Active Shooter Situation?

Anywhere that the general public is allowed access will be at risk of having an active shooter situation. Even places where the public is not allowed have experienced active shooter situations due to disgruntled employees or former employees. If your institution has a history of workplace violence, you should mark your risk assessment as high. If your collection contains any items that could be considered controversial, you should also mark your risk assessment as high.

Real-Life Examples of Active Shooters

Example #1: In August 2017, a gunman walked into a public library in eastern New Mexico on a Monday afternoon and opened fire. The gunman fatally shot two workers inside the public library and wounded four others. According to authorities, officers received a "shots fired" call around 4:13 P.M. Dispatch reported an active shooter inside the library and said two people had been shot. When officers arrived on the scene, they said they encountered the shooter who was arrested without incident. Reports indicated that the gunman told investigators he had been thinking "bad things" for some time and initially planned to target his school because he was angry that he was on a two-day suspension from Clovis High School.[31]

Example #2: On November 20, 2014, three Florida University students were shot and wounded in the school's Strozier Library by a gunman who was an alumni of the school and a lawyer. Police officials said that the shooter graduated from Florida State before attending Texas Tech University's law school. The gunman, who was troubled by personal crises and mistrust of the government, opened fire and shot three people, including two students at the entrance of the library. There were many frightened students in the university's main library when the shooting began. Many hid themselves inside the library and stacked tables and chairs against one of the entrances, while other students ran out a back exit. Several minutes after the shooting, the gunman was shot outside the library's exit by police officers. The university canceled classes and provided counseling services to students. News conferences were held throughout the day to keep the public informed of the investigation.[32]

BOMB THREAT

Most bomb threats are received either directly or indirectly by telephone. They may sometimes be received as e-mail or by postal mail. Sometimes the person issuing the bomb threat wants something, for instance, money, in exchange for not detonating a bomb, but many times they will simply declare that a bomb has been planted on your premises.

The Dangers of Bomb Threats

More often than not bomb threats are actually hoaxes, but that does not mean you should not take each and every bomb threat seriously. Bomb threats that lead to the detonation of an explosive device are dangerous to both the staff and patrons. In addition, they may cause extensive damage to the collection and to the building. Even bomb threats that turn out to be hoaxes still take time and resources away from the library staff as well as the first responders whose job it is to handle situations like these.

Is My Institution at Risk of Bomb Threats?

Any institution can receive a bomb threat. Institutions who are at highest risk of a bomb being planted on their premises are those with an inadequate security system in place. Libraries who check bags and packages, routinely sweep the premises for suspicious packages and boxes, and are observant of people roaming around the building (both inside and out) will be at the lowest risk.

Real-Life Examples of Bomb Threats

Example #1: In 2007, the Edmonds Community College library in Lynnwood, Washington, received a series of bomb threats starting about 8 A.M. The campus was evacuated and locked down for three hours while bomb-sniffing dogs searched the building for explosives. The building was reopened about 11 A.M. The calls were traced to a 16-year-old student who did not want to go to class. The individual was arrested at his parents' home.[33]

Example #2: A bomb threat occurred in April 2017 at the Cosumnes River College in Sacramento, California. Shortly afterward, students received multiple notifications alerting them of the bomb threat. The alerts stated that police had reported a bomb threat in the college's library and indicated that students should maintain their distance from the building. Classes and offices located in the library were closed, and students and staff were evacuated from the building. Officials with bomb-sniffing dogs arrived on campus and conducted a search of the library. After almost three hours of investigation, another alert was sent out to the campus stating that the police did not find a bomb and had ruled the library building as cleared and safe. According to authorities, a suspect was taken into custody because the suspect left a backpack behind in the library and had made a threat previously.[34]

Example #3: In 2015, police in Massachusetts were contacted around 5:30 P.M. by someone who claimed to be holding two hostages inside the Hopkinton Public Library. The caller claimed to have a bomb and demanded a ransom of $50,000. Businesses and residents in close proximity to the library were evacuated, and police temporarily closed the streets surrounding the area. Officers eventually swept the building and determined the library was empty. The police chief described the incident as a "swatting" call, a type of hoax intended to draw heavy police presence.[35]

HURRICANES

Hurricanes are defined as tropical cyclones with winds of 74 miles (119 kilometers) per hour (mph) or greater. Hurricanes are classified according to their intensity, with a Category 1 hurricane being the least severe with winds of 74–95 mph and a Category 5 hurricane having winds greater than 155 mph. They are formed when warm ocean water is combined with the Earth's eastward rotation.[36] The National Hurricane Center states that the average hurricane eye (the calmest part of the storm) stretches 20 to 30 miles across, but some can grow as large as 120 miles wide. In 2017, Hurricane Irma had winds up to 185 mph, and the eye of Hurricane Irma fluctuated around 30 miles across. For context, the eye was big enough to cover the small Caribbean island of Barbuda, and the entire hurricane would engulf the state of Michigan. Hurricane Irma was so large that it was clearly visible to astronauts stationed on the International Space Station.[37]

The Dangers of Hurricanes

When people think about hurricanes, the strong winds are what comes first to mind. However, there are other factors that generate major threats as well. Let's look at them in detail.

Storm Surge and Storm Tide

A storm surge occurs when the hurricane's strong winds push water into shore, and it can be considered the most dangerous part of any hurricane. Among all the hurricane-related dangers, a storm surge is the greatest potential threat to life and property. The storm surge was the main cause of death during Hurricane Katrina.[38] Other notable storm surges include Hurricane Ike, which had storm surges of 15–20 feet above normal tide levels, and Hurricane Isabel, with storm surges of more than 8 feet that flooded rivers that flowed into the bay across Virginia, Maryland, Delaware, and Washington, D.C.[39]

Heavy Rainfall and Inland Flooding

Hurricanes often produce huge amounts of rain and flooding that can be a major problem, particularly for inland communities. The average hurricane produces at least 6 to 12 inches of rain, which results in floods that cause considerable damage and loss of life, especially in mountainous areas where heavy rains mean flash floods. Flash flooding, a rapid rise in water levels, can occur quickly due to the heavy rainfall. There is also the issue of longer-term flooding on rivers and streams that can continue for several days after the hurricane. The amount of rainfall a hurricane produces is related to the speed and size of the storm as well as the geography of the area. Slower-moving and larger storms produce more rainfall. In terms of geography, mountainous terrain heightens the amount of rainfall from a hurricane.[40]

High Winds

The high winds of a hurricane can produce damage that is both substantial and costly. Winds measuring 74 mph or greater on the Saffir-Simpson Hurricane Wind Scale can destroy buildings and mobile homes. These high winds can also knock down trees and turn debris into deadly flying objects. They can also be deadly for people to be caught in, so it is best to complete all evacuations and have everyone sheltered as quickly as possible. In 2004, Hurricane Charley made landfall at Punta Gorda on the southwest Florida coast and produced major damage well inland across central Florida with gusts of more than 100 mph.[41]

Rip Currents

The strong winds of a tropical cyclone can cause dangerous waves known as rip currents, and they can pose a significant hazard to people. These channeled currents of water flow away from shore, past the line of breaking waves. Even if the hurricane is not near the coastline, these life-threatening rip currents can be a danger, as they can occur even when a hurricane is miles offshore.[42] In fact in 2008, three people were killed along New Jersey's coast from rip currents caused by Hurricane Bertha, which was more than 1,000 miles away from shore.[43] In addition, all six deaths in 2009 in the United States directly attributable to tropical cyclones occurred as the result of drowning from large waves or strong rip currents.[44]

Tornadoes

As a hurricane moves toward the shore, tornadoes often develop on the fringes of the storm. These tornadoes can cause massive amounts of destruction. Typically, the more intense a hurricane is, the greater the tornado threat.[45] In 2004, Hurricane Ivan caused an outbreak of 117 tornadoes, the largest known outbreak of hurricane-related tornadoes to date.[46]

Hurricanes versus Cyclones versus Typhoons

Hurricanes and cyclones are different names for the same weather occurrence, with the official name for this meteorological phenomenon being a tropical cyclone. The difference is in the geographical location: "hurricanes" occur in the Atlantic and Northeast Pacific, while "typhoons" occur in the Northwest Pacific, and "cyclones" occur in the South Pacific and Indian Ocean. Typhoons tend to cause less damage due to their geographic location, though typhoons can be stronger and occur more frequently than hurricanes due to the warmer Pacific Ocean waters.

Hurricane Watch versus Hurricane Warning

When a hurricane is looming, you may hear the terms "hurricane watch" and "hurricane warning." It is important to know the difference between these two terms.

A hurricane watch means that there is potential for hurricane conditions (sustained winds of 74 mph or higher) within the specified area.[47] A hurricane watch is typically issued 48 hours in advance of the anticipated onset of a hurricane. When a hurricane watch is issued, it is recommended that you undertake any necessary preparations and that you review your plan for evacuation in case a hurricane warning is issued.

A hurricane warning means that hurricane conditions are expected somewhere within the specified area.[48] A hurricane warning is typically issued 36 hours in advance of the anticipated onset of a hurricane. When a hurricane warning is issued, it is recommended that all storm preparations are completed, and if directed, all people are evacuated from the area.

Is My Institution at Risk of a Hurricane or Typhoon?

The risk of a hurricane affecting your institution will be based mostly on your location and the time of year. Historically, more hurricanes hit Florida than any other U.S. state.[49] The top five U.S. cities that are most vulnerable to hurricanes are Miami, Key West, and Tampa, Florida; Cape Hatteras, North Carolina; and New Orleans, Louisiana.[50]

Hurricane season officially runs from June 1 through November 30, but it is not unheard of to see hurricanes before and after these dates, though this is a rare occurrence. During an average hurricane season, eight to eleven tropical storms can be expected, and of these, five to seven will potentially develop into full-fledged hurricanes.[51]

Real-Life Examples of Hurricane Damage

Example #1: Sewage, water damage, and mold was the outcome of Hurricane Sandy, which caused the Shrewsbury River in New Jersey to overflow, sending 2 feet of water into the Oceanport Public Library. Because of water-damaged books, books contaminated by sewage, and a mold outbreak, the library lost its entire collection—18,000 items worth $380,000.[52]

Example #2: Four branches of the Queens Public Library were able to salvage around 50,000 books damaged by sewage and mold caused by Hurricane Sandy. It shipped its books to Rapid Refile but still ended up discarding some 100,000 books due to contamination issues.

Example #3: Island Park Public Library in Nassau County, New York, was filled with 3 feet of seawater after it was hit by Hurricane Sandy, and some sewage water caused it to lose all the items contained on the bottom two shelves of the stacks on the first floor.

Example #4: Hurricane Harvey caused extensive flooding to the University of Houston Law Library.

Example #5: The Kendall Neighborhood branch of the Houston Public Library is estimated to have taken on up to 6 feet of water as a result of flooding after Hurricane Harvey.

Example #6: The main branch and the Larry R. Jackson branch of the Lakeland Public Library was closed due to flooding in Florida after Hurricane Irma. They responded creatively by loading carts with books and DVDs, and setting up the items in front of the buildings, creating a temporary "pop-up" library.[53]

Example #7: In the Daytona Beach, Florida, Regional Branch of the Volusia County Public Library, approximately 8 inches of water flowed into the children's department during Hurricane Irma. The storm destroyed $5,000 of the library's holdings. This particular library is located on City Island in the Halifax River, which rose 3 feet due to the storm surge and flooded 80 percent of the building.[54]

Power Outages

Hurricanes are a major cause of power outages at libraries. Some power outages may be short and only affect a few places, while others may effect entire cities and last for a great deal of time.

Example #1: Elyria, Ohio, received more than 8 inches of rain from Hurricane Sandy, shutting down the power in the main branch of the public library for more than 36 hours.[55]

Example #2: More than four days after Hurricane Irma, the Coral Gables Branch Library in Coral Gables, Florida, was still without electricity.

Example #3: In addition, 100 days after Hurricane Maria half of the island of Puerto Rico was still without power, making it the longest blackout in American history.[56]

TORNADOES

A tornado is a funnel- or cone-shaped cloud with winds that can reach up to 300 mph. The funnel is made up of water droplets, dust, and debris. On average, a tornado will have a wind speed that is less than 110 mph, though winds can go up to 200–300 mph, be about 250 feet wide, and only travel about 2 to 3 miles. They may last about five minutes on the ground before dissipating.[57] An average of 1,000 tornadoes strike the United States every year.

The Dangers of Tornadoes

The destructive winds produced by tornadoes cause debris of varying size and type, including dirt, sand, and rocks, to move at extremely high speeds that can easily penetrate clothing and skin, causing very serious injuries, including death.[58] There is also the added element of danger because tornadoes can strike with little or no warning. In fact, tornadoes are considered the most violent of all storms on Earth.

Tornado Watch versus Tornado Warning

The difference between a tornado watch and a tornado warning is critical to disaster preparedness. The National Oceanic and Atmospheric Administration (NOAA) Storm Prediction Center meteorologists will issue a tornado watch when the weather conditions are favorable for tornadoes. A watch can cover parts of a state or can include several states. A tornado warning means that a funnel cloud has been sighted or that weather radar has detected the possible formation of a tornado. A tornado warning means you need to act now and seek shelter immediately. A tornado warning means imminent danger to property and the potential for serious injury and loss of life.[59]

Is My Institution at Risk of Tornadoes?

The risk of a tornado occurring in your area has to do with your location, the time of year, and the time of day. Tornadoes can happen anywhere. They have been observed on every continent with the exception of Antarctica but are most common in the area of the United States known as Tornado Alley. Though Tornado Alley has no agreed upon boundaries, it generally includes the states of Arkansas, Iowa, Illinois, Indiana, Kansas, Louisiana, Minnesota, Nebraska, North Dakota, Ohio, Oklahoma, South Dakota, and Texas. Lesser known is Dixie Alley, an area in the Gulf Coast region of the United States that has a relatively high frequency of tornadoes occurring in the late fall, October through December.[60] The timing varies with other locations.

Tornadoes are most common between the months of March and August, with the month of May historically being the most active month for tornadoes in many parts of the United States.[61] The southern plains see the most tornado activity during May into early June. The northern plains and upper Midwest see the most tornado activity in June or July. While tornadoes can occur at any time of the day, they are more likely to occur between 4 and 9 P.M. It is important to be aware of the signs that a tornado is approaching including a dark, greenish sky; large hail; a large, dark, low-lying cloud; and a loud roar like a freight train.[62] Tornadoes are fairly uncommon during the winter months because they need warm weather to form, but on occasion, a tornado is recorded during the months between December and February.

Real-Life Examples of Tornado Damage to Libraries

Example #1: The 2011 Tuscaloosa–Birmingham tornado caused varying degrees of damage to about a dozen public and school libraries in Alabama.[63] The library at the Alberta Elementary School in Tuscaloosa had to be temporarily housed at another school after the entire Alberta Elementary School building was destroyed. The librarian at this school library was forced to rebuild her collection practically from scratch. The Ragland Public Library staff in Ragland was able to salvage most of the 15,000-item collection; however, the building was ruined, and the library's eight computers were destroyed.[64]

Example #2: When a tornado hit Morehead City and Atlantic Beach in North Carolina on November 26, 2013, the library at Carteret Community College was forced to close due to structural damage found of walls and windows when an inspection was conducted by college personnel, a structural engineer, and the city's chief building inspector. The library was forced to temporarily relocate to another space on the college campus.

Example #3: On August 28, 1990, a tornado struck without warning and damaged the Plainfield Public Library branch in Plainfield, Illinois. The branch collection of over 12,000 items suffered extensive water damage. Volunteers were tasked with boxing damaged books that were then shipped to M. F. Bank, a book restoration company in Atlanta, for drying and preservation.[65]

EARTHQUAKES

An earthquake occurs when there is a sudden powerful shaking of the ground, which is caused by a sudden slip on a fault. The tectonic plates are always slowly moving, but they get stuck at their edges due to friction. When the stress on the edge overcomes the friction, there is a release of energy in waves that travels through the earth's crust and causes the shaking that we feel.[66] Aftershocks, which are simply additional earthquakes, may follow the initial earthquake. The majority of them are smaller than the initial earthquake, but larger-magnitude aftershocks are known to occur. It is estimated that 500,000 detectable earthquakes occur in the world each year, and of those, 100,000 can be felt, and 100 of them cause damage.[67]

Why Are Earthquakes Dangerous?

One of the main dangers of earthquakes is the effects of ground shaking. Ground shaking can cause severe structural damage to a building and may also cause landslides and mudslides, which can be deadly. Earthquakes can also break dams or levees along a river, and the flowing water from the river can cause severe flooding. Earthquakes have been known to damage gas lines and power lines, resulting in fires.

Is My Institution at Risk of Earthquakes?

Earthquakes can strike any location at any time, but some locations are more prone than others to have earthquakes. They generally occur in three large zones of the earth. It is estimated that 81 percent of the world's largest earthquakes occur in the world's greatest earthquake belt, the circum-Pacific seismic belt, which is found along the rim of the Pacific Ocean. This belt, also known as the Ring of Fire, extends from Chile northward along the South American coast through Central America, Mexico, and the West Coast of the United States. It continues to the southern part of Alaska, through the Aleutian Islands to Japan, the Philippine Islands, New Guinea, the island groups of the Southwest

Pacific, and New Zealand.[68] The second zone is known as the Alpide belt. This belt extends from Java to Sumatra through the Himalayas, the Mediterranean, and out into the Atlantic. Around 17 percent of the world's largest earthquakes occur in this belt, including some of the most destructive.[69] The third area is known at the Mid-Atlantic Ridge. It is a mostly underwater mountain range in the Atlantic Ocean that extends from the Arctic Ocean to near the southern tip of Africa.[70]

Because recent earthquakes are occurring in places where they were once rare, you should keep an eye out for news regarding earthquakes in your area to see if you might be at risk. An example of this is in the Dallas–Fort Worth region of Texas. The historical record shows the area might have had one earthquake in 1950; other than that there had been no recorded seismic activity until recently. Since 2008, there have been over 100 seismic events in the area known as the Fort Worth Basin. Oklahoma has also seen a rise in seismic activity. There used to be, on average, two earthquakes a year in Oklahoma that were of magnitude 3 or greater. But beginning in 2009, earthquakes started increasing more frequently. In 2013, there were 109 earthquakes, and each following year, the amount of earthquakes began increasing by the hundreds. There were 903 reports of earthquakes in 2015 alone. The rise in earthquakes in both Texas and Oklahoma is linked to man-made causes.

Within the United States, California and Alaska have the largest amount of earthquakes. Other areas that receive a good number of earthquakes include Utah, Idaho, Montana, the northern part of New York State, Missouri, South Carolina, Hawaii, and Puerto Rico. Florida and North Dakota, on the other hand, have the smallest number of earthquakes in the United States.[71]

Unlike with hurricanes or tornadoes, there is no "earthquake season." Scientists have looked for patterns in the time of year and time of day that earthquakes occur, but they have not discovered anything significant.[72] In other words, there is no particular time of year when earthquakes are more prone to occur than not. Earthquakes happen all year long, and they can happen at all hours of the day.

Real-Life Examples of Earthquakes

Example #1: On November 6, 2016, a 5.0 earthquake hit the Cushing area of Oklahoma. The earthquake damaged dozens of buildings including the Cushing Public Library. The library's walls and floors were damaged, and furniture and bookshelves were knocked over. While most of the book collection was not damaged, an antique map fell from the wall, and a collection of model ships that were donated to the library in the 1940s also suffered damage.[73]

Example #2: In 2014, a 5.1 earthquake affected the Pollak Library at California State University, Fullerton. The library was forced to be closed while repairs to the ceiling and HVAC system were performed. There was quite a bit aesthetic damage, cracked glass, and damaged furniture. Initially, the university estimated the damage on campus to be $500,000, but upon further inspection, the total was closer to $6 million.[74]

Example #3: The Delmar T. Oviatt Library at California State University, Northridge, was damaged in January 1994. Approximately 600 books had fallen from the shelves, and there was damage to the drywall on the fourth floor of the building. The library shelving was braced and reinforced and survived undamaged. A microform cabinet in the basement fell over and caused extensive damage, with half of them needing to be replaced. Exterior damage included a partial collapse of the overhanging roof, damage to two columns, and metal and concrete debris from the damage.[75]

This chapter has covered common disasters and emergencies and their potential effect on your library. The next chapter will discuss emergency procedures, prevention, response, and recovery.

NOTES

1. "Flood Basics." NOAA National Severe Storms Laboratory. Accessed January 17, 2018. https://www.nssl.noaa.gov/education/svrwx101/floods/.
2. NWS Flood Safety Home, and U.S. Department of Commerce, NOAA, National Weather Service. NWS Flood Safety Home Page. January 1, 2001. Accessed January 17, 2018. http://www.floodsafety.noaa.gov/watch_warning.shtml.
3. "Flood Basics." NOAA National Severe Storms Laboratory.
4. Stevens, Taylor. "Sugar House Library Re-opens after Devastating Flood That Destroyed Thousands of Books." *The Salt Lake Tribune.* October 23, 2017. Accessed January 17, 2018. http://www.sltrib.com/news/2017/10/23/as-sprague-library-partially-reopens-after-devastating-flood-refugee-readers-are-glad-to-return/.
5. Ortigo, Bridget. "Jefferson's Historic Carnegie Library Damaged by Flooding." *Marshall News Messenger.* November 25, 2017. Accessed January 17, 2018. https://www.marshallnewsmessenger.com/news/2017/nov/25/jeffersons-historic-carnegie-library-damaged-by-fl/.
6. Carlson, Kate. "$500K Donated to Library Flood Restoration." *Midland Daily News.* October 17, 2017. Accessed January 17, 2018. http://www.ourmidland.com/news/article/500K-donated-to-nbsp-library-flood-restoration-12283870.php.
7. Gardiner, Dustin, and Yihyun Jeong. "Burton Barr Library Damage: How Did It Happen?" *Azcentral.* July 16, 2017. Accessed January 17, 2018. https://www.azcentral.com/story/news/local/phoenix/2017/07/16/phoenix-burton-barr-library-damage-how-did-happen/482798001/.
8. Ibid.
9. Goulding, Susan Christian. "Tustin Library, Shuttered since March due to Water Damage, Opens a Temporary Indoor-Outdoor Site." *Orange County Register.* August 16, 2017. Accessed January 17, 2018. https://www.ocregister.com/2017/08/15/tustin-library-shuttered-since-march-due-to-water-damage-opens-a-temporary-indoor-outdoor-site/.
10. Hayward, Mark. "Burst Sprinkler Pipe Spells a Mess for West Side Library | New Hampshire." New Hampshire Union Leader. February 19, 2015. Accessed July 5, 2018.

http://www.unionleader.com/apps/pbcs.dll/article?AID=/20150219/NEWS07/150219054/0/news09&template=printart.

11. "Mold." Harvard Library. Accessed January 17, 2018. http://library.harvard.edu/preservation/mold.

12. Ibid.

13. "UIUC Rare Book Library Closes due to Mold." *American Libraries Magazine*. February 28, 2008. Accessed January 17, 2018. https://americanlibrariesmagazine.org/uiuc-rare-book-library-closes-due-to-mold/.

14. Logue, J. "Mold Damages Thousands of Books on Fifth Floor of McKeldin Library." *The Diamondback*. September 2, 2013. Accessed January 17, 2018. http://www.dbknews.com/archives/article_b508d354-140d-11e3-bc17-0019bb30f31a.html.

15. Ryan, Andrew. "Mold Outbreak Closes Rare Book Section at Boston Public Library." BostonGlobe.com. September 18, 2015. Accessed January 17, 2018. https://www.bostonglobe.com/metro/2015/09/18/mold-outbreak-closes-rare-book-section-boston-public-library/yYm9pVYxmUhUCBS6v8KK9O/story.html.

16. Greene, Susan. "Don't Let the Bedbooks Bite." *The Denver Post*. September 21, 2009. Accessed January 17, 2018. https://www.denverpost.com/2009/09/21/greene-dont-let-the-bedbooks-bite/.

17. "Museums Waging War on Exhibit-Eating Bugs." *BBC News*. August 31, 2011. Accessed January 17, 2018. http://www.bbc.com/news/science-environment-14630783.

18. Monir, Malak. "Qatar Museum Experts Freeze Out Uninvited Guests." *Doha News*. May 7, 2016. Accessed January 17, 2018. https://dohanews.co/qatar-museum-experts-freeze-out-uninvited-guests/.

19. "CPR Facts and Stats." Accessed January 17, 2018. http://cpr.heart.org/AHAECC/CPRAndECC/AboutCPRFirstAid/CPRFactsAndStats/UCM_475748_CPR-Facts-and-Stats.jsp.

20. "Opioid Overdose." Centers for Disease Control and Prevention. August 30, 2017. Accessed January 17, 2018. https://www.cdc.gov/drugoverdose/epidemic/index.html.

21. "Saving Lives in the Stacks." *American Libraries Magazine*. June 21, 2017. Accessed January 17, 2018. https://americanlibrariesmagazine.org/2017/06/21/saving-lives-in-the-stacks/.

22. "Partnership Prepares Library to Help Sudden Cardiac Arrest Victims." District of Columbia Public Library. May 12, 2011. Accessed January 17, 2018. https://www.dclibrary.org/node/13734.

23. Epstein, Edward. "U.S. Libraries Checking Out Book Theft/'Most-Stolen' List Will Help Curb Crime." *SFGate*. May 15, 2001. Accessed January 17, 2018. http://www.sfgate.com/news/article/U-S-libraries-checking-out-book-theft-2921164.php.

24. "What Drives People to Steal Precious Books." *Financial Times*. Accessed January 17, 2018. https://www.ft.com/content/d41a83d6-09dc-11de-add8-0000779fd2ac.

25. "Wildfires Information and Facts." *National Geographic*. January 10, 2017. Accessed January 17, 2018. https://www.nationalgeographic.com/environment/natural-disasters/wildfires/.

26. "Fire 101: The Dangers of Fire?" Purdue University. Accessed January 17, 2018. http://www.purdue.edu/ehps/fire/fire-101.html.

27. "NWS Wildland Fire Safety Watch vs. Warning Home Page." National Weather Service. January 1, 2001. Accessed January 17, 2018. http://www.nws.noaa.gov/om/fire/ww.shtml.

28. George, Eberhart M. "Electrical Fire Closes Hamline University Library." November 2000.

29. "Active Shooter Preparedness." Department of Homeland Security. May 12, 2017. Accessed January 17, 2018. https://www.dhs.gov/active-shooter-preparedness.

30. "Active Shooter Emergency Action Plan." https://www.dhs.gov/xlibrary/assets/active_shooter_booklet.pdf.

31. Associated Press. "Teen Accused in New Mexico Library Rampage Had Planned to Shoot Up School, Police Say." Chicagotribune.com. August 30, 2017. Accessed January 17, 2018. http://www.chicagotribune.com/g00/news/nationworld/ct-new-mexico-library-shooting-20170830-story.html?i10c.encReferrer=aHR0cHM6Ly93d3cuZ29vZ2xlLmNvbS8%3D&i10c.ua=1.

32. Rossman, Sean. "Shooting at Strozier Library Stuns Florida State." *Tallahassee Democrat.* November 21, 2014. Accessed January 17, 2018. http://www.tallahassee.com/story/news/local/fsu-news/2014/11/20/shooting-strozier-library-stuns-florida-state/70040320/.

33. Bureau, Times Snohomish County. "Suspect Arrested in Edmonds College Bomb Threats." *The Seattle Times.* April 19, 2007. Accessed January 17, 2018. https://www.seattletimes.com/seattle-news/suspect-arrested-in-edmonds-college-bomb-threats/.

34. Rusche, Shannon. "Police Evacuate Library due to Bomb Threat." *The Connection.* Accessed January 17, 2018. https://www.thecrcconnection.com/news/2017/04/06/police-evacuate-library-due-to-bomb-threat/.

35. Haddadin, Jim. "Hopkinton Town Center Re-opens after Bomb Threat Deemed Hoax." *MetroWest Daily News.* April 4, 2015. Accessed January 17, 2018. http://www.metrowestdailynews.com/article/20150404/news/150407929.

36. Brobst, John L., Lauren H. Mandel, and Charles R. Mcclure. "Public Libraries and Crisis Management: Roles of Public Libraries in Hurricane/Disaster Preparedness and Response." Crisis Information Management. 2012.

37. Kettley, Sebastian. "Hurricane Irma: How Big Is the Hurricane and How Wide Is the Eye of the Storm?" Express.co.uk. September 6, 2017. Accessed January 17, 2018. https://www.express.co.uk/news/weather/850773/Hurricane-Irma-how-big-wide-is-Irma-eye-storm-map-NOAA-NHC-size-forecast.

38. Ellis, Sam. "Why a Storm Surge Can Be the Deadliest Part of a Hurricane." *Vox.* September 9, 2017. Accessed January 17, 2018. https://www.vox.com/2017/9/9/16278822/storm-surge-deadliest-part-irma-hurricane.

39. "Storm Surge Overview." Accessed January 17, 2018. http://www.nhc.noaa.gov/surge/#EVENTS.

40. "Hurricane Preparedness—Hazards." Accessed January 17, 2018. http://www.nhc.noaa.gov/prepare/hazards.php.

41. Ibid.

42. "5 Deadliest Hurricane-Related Dangers." Local Weather from AccuWeather.com—Superior Accuracy™. Accessed January 17, 2018. https://www.accuweather.com/en/weather-news/5-of-the-deadliest-hurricane-dangers/70001646.

43. Ibid.

44. "Hurricane Preparedness—Hazards."

45. Ibid.

46. Lam, Linda. "The Overlooked Side of Harvey: Tornadoes." The Weather Channel. September 15, 2017. Accessed January 17, 2018. https://weather.com/storms/hurricane/news/hurricane-harvey-tornado-reports.

47. U.S. Department of Commerce, National Oceanic and Atmospheric Administration. "What Is the Difference between a Hurricane Watch and a Warning?" NOAA's

National Ocean Service. June 28, 2013. Accessed January 17, 2018. https://oceanser vice.noaa.gov/facts/watch-warning.html.

48. Ibid.

49. Brobst et al., "Public Libraries and Crisis Management."

50. "Top 5 US Cities Most Vulnerable to Hurricanes." Local Weather from AccuWeather. com—Superior Accuracy™. Accessed January 17, 2018. https://www.accuweather.com/ en/weather-news/top-5-most-vulnerable-us-cities-to-hurricanes-atlantic-tropical-sea son/48281135.

51. Landsea, Chris. "How Many Tropical Cyclones Have There Been Each Year in the Atlantic Basin?" Atlantic Oceanographic and Meteorological Laboratories. Accessed January 17, 2018. http://www.aoml.noaa.gov/hrd/tcfaq/E11.html.

52. Manuel, John. "The Long Road to Recovery: Environmental Health Impacts of Hurricane Sandy." *Environmental Health Perspectives* no. 5 (2013), 121–152.

53. Guinn, Christopher. "Lakeland's 'Popup' Library Makes Most of Situation." *The Ledger.* September 14, 2017. Accessed January 17, 2018. http://www.theledger.com/ news/20170914/lakelands-popup-library-makes-most-of-situation.

54. Eberhart, George M. "Hurricanes Harvey and Irma." *American Libraries Magazine.* October 30, 2017. Accessed January 17, 2018. https://americanlibrariesmagazine .org/2017/11/01/hurricanes-harvey-irma-libraries/.

55. Manuel, "The Long Road to Recovery."

56. Sputnik. "The Forgotten: Half of Puerto Rico without Power 100 Days after Hurricane Maria." *Sputnik International.* December 23, 2017. Accessed January 17, 2018. https://sputniknews.com/latam/201712241060275866-half-puerto-rico-without-power-hurricane-maria/.

57. "General Tornado Facts." Educational Tornado Facts and Information. Accessed January 17, 2018. http://www.tornadofacts.net/general-tornado-facts.php.

58. Ohio Committee for Severe Weather Awareness (OCSWA), "Tornado Safety & the Dangers of Highway Overpasses." Ohio.gov, Accessed January 17, 2018. http://www .weathersafety.ohio.gov/TornadoSafety.aspx.

59. "Tornado Safety Facts." Tornado Safety Facts and Tornado Safety 101. Accessed January 17, 2018. http://www.tornadofacts.net/tornado-safety-facts.php#watch-vs-warning.

60. "Tornado Basics." NOAA National Severe Storms Laboratory. Accessed January 17, 2018. http://www.nssl.noaa.gov/education/svrwx101/tornadoes/.

61. "General Tornado Facts." Educational Tornado Facts and Information.

62. "Tornadoes." Ready.gov. Accessed January 17, 2018. https://www.ready.gov/tornadoes.

63. Wolfson, Hannah. "Tornado-Damaged Alabama Libraries Get Help." AL.com. July 5, 2011. Accessed January 17, 2018. http://blog.al.com/spotnews/2011/07/tornado-damaged_alabama_librar.html.

64. Ibid.

65. "Tornado History." Plainfield Public Library. Accessed January 17, 2018. https:// plainfieldpubliclibrary.org/resources/tornado-history/.

66. "What Is an Earthquake and What Causes Them to Happen?" Accessed January 17, 2018. https://www.usgs.gov/faqs/what-earthquake-and-what-causes-them-happen? qt-news_science_products=7#qt-news_science_products.

67. "Earthquakes." Ready.gov. Accessed January 17, 2018. https://www.ready.gov/earthquakes.

68. "Where Do Earthquakes Occur?" Accessed January 17, 2018. https://www.usgs.gov/faqs/ where-do-earthquakes-occur?qt-news_science_products=7—qt-news_science_products.

69. Ibid.

70. The Editors of Encyclopædia Britannica. "Mid-Atlantic Ridge." *Encyclopædia Britannica.* April 15, 2010. Accessed January 17, 2018. https://www.britannica.com/place/Mid-Atlantic-Ridge.

71. Villaverde, Roberto. *Fundamental Concepts of Earthquake Engineering.* Boca Raton, FL: CRC, 2009.

72. Jones, Lucy. "Caltech Science Question of the Month: Is there Earthquake Weather or an Earthquake Hour?" The California Institute of Technology. Accessed January 17, 2018. http://www.caltech.edu/news/caltech-science-question-month-there-earthquake-weather-or-earthquake-hour-43.

73. Young, Bill. "Cushing Public Library Suffers Earthquake Damage." ODL News Blog. November 15, 2016. Accessed January 17, 2018. http://news.oklibshare.org/oklahoma-public-libraries/cushing-public-library-suffers-earthquake-damage/.

74. "Repairs to CSUF Library after Earthquake Could Cost More Than $6 Million." *Daily Titan.* May 5, 2014. Accessed January 17, 2018. https://dailytitan.com/2014/04/repairs-to-csuf-library-after-earthquake-could-cost-more-than-6-million/

75. "Oviatt Library Earthquake Damage." Oviatt Library. Accessed January 17, 2018. https://library.csun.edu/About/Quake.

CHAPTER 3

Emergency Procedures: Prevention, Response, and Recovery

This chapter covers the most effective ways to prevent, respond, and recover from common disasters and emergencies. In general, you should always remember that safety always comes first. Your first priority is the safety of the library staff and its patrons and then the safety of the collections and the building. The procedures listed here should only be done if it is safe to do so. The health and safety coordinator should always assess the health and safety risks of every phase of emergency response. These guidelines are a foundation for you to create your own emergency procedures, to take and customize for your library. That is, eliminate procedures that are not applicable to your institution or add more information where necessary; for example, add the specific exits to use in an evacuation.

WATER-RELATED DISASTERS

Prevention

Most instances of flooding happen on the lowest and highest floors of a building; basements are always the first to flood, and the top floors are the first to be affected by leaking or damaged roofs. Because of this, one of the best ways to prevent water-related damage is to try to avoid placing collection items in these areas. Other places to avoid storing your collection include any area that is located on an exterior wall, as these spaces are more likely to gather moisture.

Regular inspections of the roof, gutters, plumbing, and windows are the key to preventing water disasters related to structural damage. The roof should be checked yearly for leaks, missing shingles, or water pooling. Sometimes water pools on flat roofs, so drainage is especially important to consider when it comes to dealing with these particular types of roofs. Be certain that any drains and gutters are checked seasonally and that they are clear and functional, not clogged with debris. A clogged gutter will cause water to pour down the side of your building, damaging both the siding and foundation. If gutters are sagging, they should be repaired. Downspouts should be extended at least 10 feet away from the building. Make sure that whoever handles the landscaping outside your building does not place compost or leaf piles against the outside walls. Communicate with them that landscape features should not include soil or any other bedding material mounded up against the walls. Vines should also be kept off all exterior walls because they can help open cracks in the siding, which allows moisture or insects to enter the house.

Inside the building, you should look for dark spots under pipes and on ceilings; these dark spots are an indicator of water damage. Also check for leaking faucets, dripping or "sweating" pipes, and faulty water drainage systems. When any deterioration or other issues are noted, it should be documented and reported to a supervisor so that repairs can be made and any future insurance claims will not be rejected. If an insurance provider discovers that you were aware of roof damage and did nothing to fix the issue and then months later a hurricane rips off a part of your roof and you suffer serious water damage, your claim will most likely be denied.

Even storing your collection items as little as 4 inches off the ground will help to protect them from floods and standing water. If shelving is unavailable, use pallets as an alternative. Wood pallets may run the risk of becoming a home to unwanted pests; if at all possible, plastic pallets are preferable. Knowing the location of nearby water sources is important when assessing the risk water might do to a collection.

When a flood watch or warning is in effect, the best way to prevent water damage to your collection is to move items to a designated safe area as soon as possible. The safe area should be located above ground on a middle floor and in a space where there are no windows or exterior walls. If your library is considered at high risk for flooding, invest in a sump pump which you can use to drain standing water.

Response

If flooding is noticeable in the building, then the disaster team should determine the exact location and source of the water. You may need to contact custodial staff or facilities management to help you with this, so have their contact information handy. If warranted, the disaster plan should be enacted by the team leader, and for safety reasons, patrons and staff should also be evacuated from any areas affected by the flooding; when water mixes with electrical systems, the results could be fatal. If the water source is determined to be coming from below, then the salvage coordinator should move the collections to higher shelves or place them on book carts and move them to a dry area when it is safe to do so.

If a flood watch or warning has been issued, then the team leader should enact the disaster plan. Someone should be assigned to watch local television, listen to radio, and monitor the Internet and social media for updates and get in contact with authorities when necessary. The team should be well versed in the different weather warnings and know the difference between a flood watch and flood warning. If water has not yet reached your facility, then it is the time to set up temporary barriers like sandbags in front of doors that may allow water to enter. If you notice water rising quickly, immediately move to higher ground. If it appears you will have to evacuate the building, make sure to turn off all the utilities at the main power source. If you have been practicing your drills regularly, you should know exactly how long it will take to evacuate the building. Do not walk through moving water; find any alternative way. Though it might not seem like much, as little as 6 inches of water can knock a person off his or her feet. Do not go into any room where the electrical outlets or electrical cords are submerged or covered by water. If you see sparks or hear buzzing, crackling, snapping, or popping noises, leave the area as quickly as possible.

If roads have begun to flood, then you will need to remain in place until the flood waters recede. Driving in flooded areas is extremely dangerous. As little as 1 foot of water can cause a car to float. In this situation, evacuate to a safe area in the library or, if necessary, to another building a short walking distance away.

Recovery

The first task to begin recovery after a flood is to have the operations coordinator call your insurance provider. The insurance provider's contact information, the policy number, and a copy of the policy should all be contained within the disaster plan. If your library was evacuated, you will want to wait until officials have stated that the building is safe to reenter. Wait until an electrician has inspected your system for safety before you turn any power on.

Before entering the area, the disaster team should be outfitted in the proper safety gear. The salvage coordinator and assistants should use the floor plan to reach all the items on the salvage priority list. These items should then be placed in a space that has been set up for salvage. For more information on how to salvage objects, see Chapter 5, "Salvage Procedures."

Be careful when walking around your library after a flood, since there will most likely be debris present and steps and floors may be slippery. The health and safety coordinator should be looking out for any of these types of hazards.

The documentation coordinator should be in charge of documenting all the damage done to the collection and the building. As stated before, it is recommended that the documentation coordinator have at least two assistants: one for photographing and/or recording and one for writing while the documentation coordinator verbally points out the damage. Cameras that are used should have a strap around them so that they do not fall into the water. Clipboards that are used to write down information should have a writing instrument attached by a string so that it too does not accidentally fall into the water.

The documentation coordinator should work with the salvage coordinator to photograph and document all the items listed on the salvage priority list. As the salvage coordinator begins to move these items to a salvage area, the documentation coordinator should make sure that there is documentation for all items being moved and where they are going. A salvage relocation form should be used here. After this task is completed, the documentation coordinator can focus on recording the damage of the rest of the collection and the building as well. A report should be put together and passed off to the operations coordinator.

The communications coordinator should be in communication with the operations coordinator and the salvage coordinator to have a better grasp on the recovery situation. Communication will have to be made with staff members who are not on the disaster team, administrators, patrons, press, and media. See Chapter 4, "Communication Procedures," for more information. The recovery process is completed when the building and the collection are both in working order.

MOLD

Prevention

The main way to prevent a mold outbreak is to control the humidity. The amount of moisture in the air is the most important environmental factor to control. Relative humidity levels should be below 50 percent. Controlling the temperature is next on the list for mold prevention. Most molds thrive in warm environments. When combined with high relative humidity, temperatures higher than 70°F can cause mold to develop. Some molds have the capability to grow in cooler climates, but the types of mold that are most commonly found in libraries tend grow less quickly in cooler temperatures. Having adequate air circulation is another way to prevent mold. When the air circulates properly, it can control mold growth because it helps to control moisture through evaporation. The easiest way to control all of the environmental factors is to have a well-designed and maintained heating, ventilation, and air-conditioning (HVAC) system with humidity control. If your library is located in a warm climate, have the HVAC system cleaned on a regular basis, even if no mold is found in the collection. It is not uncommon for mold to form in drainage pans and pipes. Chapter 2 explained the real-life example of the mold outbreak at University of Maryland's McKeldin Library in 2013. Though the library staff were aware of high relative humidity issues causing the mold outbreak, there were no plans at the time to replace the underperforming HVAC system. A few years later, they experienced more mold issues in the library and are now working to replace the system.

Choosing the best location for your collection can also help prevent mold. It is best not to shelve books directly against an outside wall. Because of differences in outside and inside temperatures, moisture may develop in or along the wall. Instead, allow air to circulate along the wall to enable evaporation. Another good way to mitigate a mold outbreak is to regularly inspect your collections for mold. This allows you to catch any contaminated items before they taint other materials and cause a mold outbreak. Continue to monitor for mold as an indicator of the environmental conditions in your library. If your library accepts book donations, then you will need to check them for mold and quarantine them for 72 hours before adding them to the rest of the collection.

Response

Identify mold correctly; if you see something that looks like mold, do not panic just yet. Mold can be any color, and foxing, dirt, dust, and stains are often mistaken for mold. To figure out whether you have mold or not, you will need to understand the characteristics of mold. There are two types of mold: active and inactive (or dormant) mold. Active mold appears as hair-like filaments in webs but then has a bushier appearance as it matures. Active mold is soft and may smear when touched with a fine brush. Active mold may also appear slimy and damp. Inactive or dormant mold poses no immediate danger to collections, but it can be spread through handling. Air currents, in favorable environmental conditions, allow mold to grow. In other words, while dormant mold may not seem dangerous, it only takes a rise in relative humidity and/or temperature to turn active. Inactive mold will appear dry and powdery, and it will easily brush off materials with little to no smearing. Even if you know the difference between these two types, it can be difficult to determine if mold is active or dormant. If there is doubt, for safety's sake, you should assume the mold is active.

Most libraries will call in a mycologist (a biologist who specializes in fungi) or some other mold specialist to determine if what they have is in fact mold. If your library does not have the funds to hire a professional to help, do not let your situation sit unresolved. An easy way to detect if the mystery matter you see is mold is to use an instant mold test. You can buy these tests at any home improvement store. The way the tests work is that you swab the matter in question and the swab instantly turns one color to show that mold is present or will turn another color, which means there is no mold present. If your mold test indicates that no mold is present, then you most likely have simply misidentified some dust or dirt. You just saved yourself the expense of calling in a mycologist. However, if your test shows that mold is present, you will now need to call a mycologist or mold specialist to help determine if the mold you have is toxic or not. If your library is on a college or university campus, consider reaching out to the Biology Department to see if they can help. Chapter 5 discusses how to remove mold from collection items. However, if you have toxic mold, you will not be able to remove the mold yourself; you will need to leave it to professionals.

Secure your collection by isolating affected materials or quarantine the affected area. If you have a small amount of items, try to place them in gallon-size freezer bags to isolate the item and prevent the mold from spreading. If you have a larger amount of items, the best option is to block off access to the area.

Assess the situation and determine how this mold outbreak occurred. The most likely culprit will be a leaking roof, leaking pipes, a flooded basement, blocked gutters, or an inefficient HVAC system. You must get to the root of the problem here, or the mold outbreak will never go away.

Recovery

You can salvage your collection's items from a mold outbreak if the mold is nontoxic or the outbreak is small enough for your staff to manage. As mentioned in the preceding paragraph, when your mold is not toxic, you can salvage the affected items in your collection yourself. The outbreak should be small enough for your staff to manage, and you need enough space to create an adequate storage area. Otherwise you will most likely have to call in a professional to handle the situation. For specific instructions on how to salvage items contaminated with mold, see Chapter 5.

If you were able to successfully salvage any collection items after a mold outbreak, the documentations coordinator should be in charge of making sure that salvaged items are marked in some way. The reasoning behind this is that while it may appear mold removal was successful, sometimes mold spores might be missed, and once these items go back into circulation, there is always a chance that a mold outbreak could reoccur. To mitigate the chances of another mold outbreak, you need to keep an eye on the materials that previously contained mold. Options include making a notation in the catalog for each item that has been treated for mold. List the date the item was treated. The salvaged items should be periodically inspected for a year from the date of treatment. Another idea is inserting a note in the item with a notice to the patron informing them that the item has been treated for mold, and if they notice any signs of mold, they should report it to the circulation desk.

PESTS

Prevention

The best way to prevent a pest infestation is to practice integrated pest management (IPM). IPM strategies encourage ongoing maintenance and housekeeping to ensure that pests will not find a hospitable environment in a library or archives building. A lot of IPM is just common sense and good housekeeping practices.

Activities include:

- Building inspection and maintenance
- Climate control
- Restriction of food and plants
- Regular cleaning
- Proper storage
- Control over incoming collections to avoid infestation of existing collections
- Routine monitoring for pests using sticky traps

One of the goals of IPM is to make the library inhospitable to pests. The idea here is that if there is no infestation, you will be less likely to have one because conditions are not favorable to most pests. This can mainly be accomplished by lowering the temperature (below 70°F) and relative humidity (not higher than 50%). Even if you already have an infestation, lowering temperature and relative humidity can cause the life cycles of insects to slow down, meaning they will breed less often, allowing you to maintain some sort of control over the situation.

Other preventative measures include discarding old boxes immediately. Leaving boxes around provides the perfect home for pests. Collapse and remove all boxes from the library the same day as they are received. Restricting food to the kitchen or break room can also deter pests. This means staff should be encouraged to eat their snacks and meals away from their desks. If any food is kept in the work area, it should be contained in at least two containers. A granola bar for example should be in a wrapper and then placed in a piece of Tupperware. The double container method prevents pests from easily accessing food. Send out monthly memo reminders or have a flyer posted in a highly visible area reminding staff to either practice the double container method or restrict food to one specific area of the building.

Response

IPM practice also has procedures for how to respond should pest infestation occur. If you find yourself with a pest infestation, you should first respond by monitoring the pests. You can do this by identifying all doors, windows, water and heat sources, and furniture on a building floor plan and checking those areas for pest activity. Be on the lookout for nesting areas, food sources, water sources, and access points.

After your initial examination, identify likely pest routes, add traps to these locations, and mark trap locations on your floor plan. Number and date the traps, and inspect and collect the traps regularly. Check the traps 48 hours after placement to see the most seriously affected areas. If the traps are coming up empty, relocate the traps elsewhere.[1] Use the pest trap log provided at the end of this chapter to help you keep track of any pest activity.

You can choose from the three main categories of traps: snap traps, live traps, and glue boards. Snap traps, used mostly for rodents, make use of a trigger-induced killing mechanism. Upon being triggered by the presence of a rodent feeding on bait, the mechanism instantly snaps shut onto the mouse or rat, killing the rodent. There are different sizes of traps—larger ones for rats and smaller models for mice. Live capture traps for rodents are also available, but they leave the unpleasant job of killing the rodents to you. Glue boards are also an option. These are helpful in that they not only trap rodents but can also retain rodent hairs and fecal pellets of escaped rodents, allowing you to monitor the presence of rodents. Glue boards do not kill mice or rats so should be inspected often in order to prevent unnecessary suffering of the trapped rodents. Glue boards are also the most likely trap to use to trap insects. Whichever trap you choose, once pests have been trapped, they must be identified to determine what threat they pose to collections.

Recovery

Using the strategies of IPM, pest infestation can be successfully prevented. If you already have an infestation, you can still use IPM strategies to eliminate the problem. However, you will run into issues if pest infestation has lingered for too long. If rodents or moths have chewed through your collection, or if insects have heavily stained your items, recovery of the collection materials will be almost impossible.

MEDICAL EMERGENCIES

Prevention

While library staff might not be able to prevent most medical emergencies from occurring, with a little preparedness, they can minimize the damage done. Library staff who learn and perform cardiopulmonary resuscitation (CPR) can double or triple a person's chance of survival, especially if performed in the first few minutes of cardiac arrest.[2] Library staff members with severe medical issues should inform their supervisors and coworkers of their situation and what signs to look for and the standard emergency treatment for the medical issue. For libraries affected by the opioid crisis, it can be helpful for staff to learn how to recognize an opioid user. The World Health Organization says that an opiate overdose can be identified by three symptoms: pinpoint pupils, unconsciousness, and respiratory depression.

Response

For minor injuries, patrons 18 years of age or older should be asked if they want to contact a family member and receive first aid. If first aid is refused, the injured person should be asked to sign an accident report stating that he or she voluntarily refused medical treatment (see example in Figure 3.1). First aid will be provided only by trained persons. In the event of occurrence of any injury requiring first aid, 911 may be called. Do not move any injured person unless there is an immediate threat to his or her life, and even then move the victim no more than necessary.

In the event a staff member, patron, or any other person on the library's property has a life-threatening medical emergency, staff should immediately call 911. Try to remain calm and speak as clearly as possible stating your name, the nature and severity of the medical problem, and your location. If the injured person is unconscious, look for a Medic-Alert or other medical ID tag.

Library staff without specialized training should only keep the sick or injured person comfortable and protected from needless disturbance until medical help arrives. Observe standard precautions and try your best to avoid contact with body fluids including blood. Since each case is unique, staff members should use their own judgment to do what is prudent and reasonable. No medication, including aspirin, should ever be dispensed to the public.[3] If a person in the building identifies himself or herself as a medical professional and offers assistance, it is advised that library staff neither encourage nor discourage treatment of the injured person.

Recovery

After a medical emergency, staff should file all necessary reports that are required by the library, such as incident reports or accident forms. A meeting should be held with the disaster team to discuss the emergency, who was effected by the incident, and how it was handled. If the same type of medical emergency keeps occurring, for example, drug overdoses, the risk assessment coordinator should take note of this and update the library's risk assessment profile. Then, the coordinator informs the disaster team.

THEFT

Prevention

Proper security is the main way to prevent theft in your library. All staff and patrons should be passed through security when entering and exiting, and all entry points to the library should have adequate and functioning alarms. Designated staff or guards should be given responsibility for inspecting bags and other materials carried into and out of the library. All staff members should know what to do when it appears that a patron has attempted to exit the building with an improperly checked-out book. Any rare items and those of considerable value should be kept in locked rooms or in locked or alarmed cases. In addition, displays in public areas should be arranged so that missing items can be readily noticed.

Valuable equipment should be bolted to desks or secured in safe places after hours. There should also be a schedule for checking inventory on a regular basis. It is also helpful to make sure that any master keys to the building are clearly marked "Do Not Duplicate" to avoid a potential thief making a copy of a master key and gaining access to the library. Be prudent about giving keys to staff; not every staff member needs access to the areas where your most valuable items are stored. Coordinate with custodial staff to have periodic maintenance and repair of locks on the library's doors.

If you have a reading room in your special collections department, make sure that there is a place for all researchers to hang their coats and bags away from the area; these items should never be brought to the desks or tables. All researchers should sign in and provide identification such as a school identification card, driver's license, or passport. Make a photocopy of the identification. In the event an item is later found to be missing, the photocopied identification card can be passed on to the authorities. Never let researchers choose their seating; you should choose their seating, and they should be placed as far apart as possible, with at least one seat in between each other. Do not allow notebooks because items can easily be slid in between their pages; provide them with paper instead.

For items that are in circulation, consider keeping your most-frequently stolen items on a shelf that is only accessible to the library staff. This forces the person to interact with the staff member in order to retrieve the item, and this lessens the chance of theft.

Response

Once an item has been found to be stolen, library staff should immediately check their records to see who the last person was who was loaned the material. Archives and special collections should look at their reading room logs to locate a name and then match it up to the photocopied identification cards on file. A report should be filed with the local police department especially if the item is rare or has a high value. A report should also be made with the database stolen-book.org, and the communication coordinator should make sure that an e-mail goes out to all rare book dealers within a 50-mile radius informing them of the item that was stolen.

Recovery

Recovering stolen items can be an extremely hard process if there is a lack of documentation. To increase your success rate of retrieving stolen property, your best bet is to look for ways to improve your security so that you can report the item missing immediately. Most libraries do not figure out that an item is stolen until well after the fact. At that point, the item is most likely not even in the possession of the thief who has already sold it on the black market or to an uninformed antiquities or rare book dealer. Thieves of rare books and manuscripts are known to have sold their stolen acquisitions in a matter of a few hours. You will also want to make sure all of your items are properly cataloged and documented in some way as your library's property to increase your chances of successful retrieval.

FIRE-RELATED DISASTERS

Prevention

All fire extinguishers are to be checked annually by a certified professional and monthly by staff to ensure the extinguisher is operational. The library staff should familiarize themselves with the location of fire extinguishers and know how to use them. Check the electrical cords throughout your building for signs of fraying, and do not overload extension cords or wall sockets. Check that your smoke alarms are in working order. Sprinkler systems should also be checked to make sure they are in working order.

When it comes to averting arson, preventing unauthorized entry into the library is the best way to stop an arsonist. The easiest points of entry are doors and windows, so make sure these are well maintained and their locks are in working order. To mitigate the potential fire damage, library staff should ensure that all doors are closed at night. Doing these checks will help contain any fire or smoke or, at the least, slow down the rate of fire growth. If you have fire-resistant areas in the library, use these areas to store any valuable items.

Response

When there are visible flames, visible smoke, smell of smoke, unusual heat, or other indications of fire, the nearest fire alarm should be pulled, and 911 should be called. If the blaze is small, attempt to extinguish it using the nearest fire extinguisher. Retrieve the nearest fire extinguisher, and follow the "P.A.S.S." procedure:

P = Pull the pin breaking the plastic seal
A = Aim at the base of the fire
S = Squeeze the handles together
S = Sweep from side to side

Inform the disaster team leader of what was witnessed and enact the disaster plan. Evacuate the building, checking all rooms for people, and close all doors and windows as you proceed to the exit. Remember not to use the elevator during a fire; use only stairwells.

Recovery

The operations coordinator should call the library's insurance provider to begin the claims process. The fire department should give the all clear before anyone returns inside the building. The salvage coordinator and any others entering the building should have the proper safety gear on. After a fire, you are often left with the destructive effects of smoke and water as well as fire damage. To remove the residual smoke, turn on fans and open windows to get the air moving. If the weather is warm, you should not open the windows, as this may drive up the humidity in the library. Instead, use a dehumidifier to help with air circulation. If there is a lot of loose ash or other debris that could become airborne and be harmful, do not turn on fans and open windows until this has been dealt with.

ACTIVE SHOOTER

Prevention

You can use quite a few approaches to prevent an active shooter situation: visual weapons screening, pattern matching, and anonymous reporting systems. The first, visual weapons screening, involves training personnel how to look for and recognize a variety of specific weapons. This approach has also been used to successfully prevent a number of planned campus shootings.

The second, pattern matching and recognition, involves training people to pay attention to patterns of human behavior that appear out of place. While these behaviors are often somewhat subtle, they can help the library staff detect potentially dangerous people regardless of the type of weapon they possess.

The final approach is to set up an anonymous reporting system for anyone to use. Simply set up a phone number with an independent third party that can be called 24/7, 365 days a year, where patrons or staff members can call to leave a brief anonymous report about suspicious behavior they have witnessed. There are a variety of vendors who provide this service and also offer web and mobile applications in addition to a telephone hotline. These can help you avoid an active shooter situation, suicides, and other deadly situations.[4]

Many active shooters give off numerous warning signs to those who interact with them on a regular basis. Therefore, it is important to build a workplace environment where the library staff members are allowed to discuss suspicious behaviors and activities with human resources without fear of retaliation or ruining someone's reputation.[5]

Response

At the first sign of an active shooter, you should run and escape if possible. During your practice drills, you should have practiced various escape routes; try to recall one of the routes you have practiced, and use it to escape. Reacting quickly is the key to survival here so leave your belongings behind. If others are with you and they can safely follow, you should proceed to escape together. If certain individuals refuse to follow you to evacuate, you should still proceed to evacuate anyway. Keep your hands visible in case law enforcement arrive on the scene. If there is no time to run or no place to run to safely, then you should hide in an area out of the shooter's view. Block the entry to your hiding place and lock any doors. Silence your cell phone or any other personal electronics so that you do not draw attention to yourself. When you have reached a safe area, call 911 and describe the shooter(s), the location where you saw the shooter(s) last, and a description of the type and quantity of weapons. If you do not have access to a call phone or landline, try putting a handwritten sign in a window. If there are any wounded people present, place direct pressure on the wound and use tourniquets if you have been trained to do so. If they are unconscious, turn them onto their sides and keep them warm. Stay in place until law enforcement gives you the all clear.

If you are unable to run or hide, then you may choose to fight as a last resort. Be prepared to cause severe or lethal injury to the shooter. If there are others around, work together to ambush the shooter with makeshift weapons like chairs, fire extinguishers, scissors, and books to distract and disarm the shooter.[6] When law enforcement arrives, your hands should be kept visible and empty. Follow law enforcement's instructions, and evacuate in the direction instructed by them.

Recovery

An active shooter situation can be traumatic for everyone involved and the community at large. If there were serious injuries and/or fatalities, a grief counselor should be made available to the staff, patrons, and anyone who wishes to talk to someone. The communications coordinator should send out a notice informing staff and patrons of the situation and allow community discussion to take place to help the healing process.

BOMB THREAT

Prevention

The best way to prevent a bomb from being planted is to have highly visible security patrol. Ideally, you want to have a security officer both inside and outside your building, but if you can only have one, then have the security office remain inside and install closed-circuit television cameras to cover the building's exterior perimeters. Sometimes bombs are left in cars to detonate, so it is suggested that you restrict any parking within 300 feet of the library. If that is not possible, attempt to arrange for employee-only vehicles to be parked closest to your building. Finally, all library staff should be properly trained so that they know what to do in the event a bomb threat is received.

Response

If you receive a bomb threat by telephone, keep the caller on the line as long as possible so that the call may be traced. Be sure not to transfer the call or interrupt the caller. Use the bomb threat form (see example in Figure 3.2) to gather as much information as possible. While you are on the phone with the caller, have someone nearby call 911. Do not hang up until directed to do so by the emergency personnel. When a bomb threat is received via a handwritten or typed note, you should handle the note as minimally as possible and call the local police department or dial 911. If a bomb threat is sent via e-mail, do not delete the message, and call the local police department or dial 911. Bombs may also be sent in the mail. Keep an eye out for unexpected packages that have no return address, excessive postage, stains, strange odors, strange sounds, misspelled words, poor handwriting, and foreign postage.[7]

Recovery

If a bomb threat is deemed to be a hoax, and the authorities have arrived, they will handle the situation from this point. Be cooperative with law enforcement while they investigate the case. The risk assessment coordinator should add this incident to the library's history profile and reevaluate the level of risk and update the disaster plan if necessary.

If a bomb goes off in your library, make sure that first responders have given the all clear before entering the building. After a bomb explosion, your collection may be damaged by fire or even water; the bomb may have caused the sprinklers to go off. Follow the salvage procedures described in Chapter 5.

HURRICANES

Damage Prevention

If your library is located in a city that is at high risk for hurricanes, consider installing hurricane shutters or hurricane-resistant windows. While these types of windows can be pricey, they will offer great protection during the hurricane season. Some insurance providers may lower your premium costs if you have these types of windows installed. Have the operations coordinator look into this if you are considering installing hurricane-resistant windows. Keep the area around your library clear of dead or rotting trees and branches that could fall during a hurricane. Librarians in hurricane-prone areas should attempt to secure their shelving to the wall and fasten any furniture to the floor.

Before hurricane season starts, the disaster team should run through the hurricane tabletop exercises and practice drills in Chapter 6 to get prepared. This will give you an opportunity to review evacuation procedures, hurricane danger signs, and first aid techniques and double check if you have sufficient emergency supplies on hand.

Response

During a hurricane warning, the health and safety coordinator should remind the disaster team of the evacuation routes. If the library is located in a low-lying area, you will need to evacuate. If the library is sturdy, on high ground, and if desired, some staff may remain during the hurricane, but they must remain indoors for the duration of the storm.[8] Anyone who remains in the building during the hurricane should stay away from all windows and exterior doors.

If your windows have protective shutters or panels, put these in place. If not, tape the windows to prevent shattered glass from being propelled into the room. Seal off any areas where water might enter the building, and put down sandbags or other temporary barriers. If it is safe to go outside, tie down any lose objects or bring them indoors. The majority of injuries during a hurricane are cuts caused by flying glass or other debris.

Recovery

If the library has suffered damage due to hurricane, the operations coordinator should contact the library's insurance provider. The insurance provider's contact information, the policy number, and a copy of the policy should all be contained within the disaster plan. If the hurricane was declared a major disaster by the U.S. government, then you should apply for FEMA aid to help you in your recovery. Declaring a major disaster provides a wide range of federal assistance programs for both individuals and the public infrastructure, including funds for both emergency and permanent work.[9]

Hurricanes can cause a lot of structural damage and flooding, so it is important to wait to enter your library until it has been deemed safe to do so. The salvage coordinator and anyone else who is entering the building should be prepared to deal with water and fallen debris, so make sure the proper safety gear is worn. Because hurricanes can cause an increase in mosquitos, any exposed skin should be sprayed with insect repellant. Everything listed on the salvage priority list should be located with the help of the floor plan included in the disaster plan. The documentation coordinator should work with the salvage coordinator to make sure all items being salvaged have been properly documented. The operations coordinator should work with the salvage coordinator to make sure any supplies that are needed are available and replenished as needed. Depending on the severity of the hurricane, electricity may be down from a few hours to a few months. The library may have to reach out to the community to find a temporary space or may have to shut down completely until all utilities can be restored. The communications coordinator will need to make contact with all library employees as well as patrons to keep them updated on the situation.

TORNADOES

Damage Prevention

Libraries in areas that are high risk for tornadoes should not have any objects outside the building unless always tied down or secured in some other way; tornadoes give very little warning, so there most likely won't be time to secure these objects beforehand. For instance, trash cans should be locked with cables or chains attached to ground anchors so that they are secure. Trees should also be regularly trimmed to minimize damage.

Before tornado season starts, the disaster team should run through the tornado tabletop exercises and practice drills to get prepared. This will give you an opportunity to review evacuation procedures, tornado danger signs, and first aid techniques and double check if you have sufficient emergency supplies on hand.

Response

During a tornado watch, windows that are on the side of the library away from the tornado's approach should be opened to equalize the air pressure. The items in your salvage priority list should be moved to an interior location. Next, move any collections that are near exterior windows to an interior location as well. If possible, all computers should be shut down during this time period. Make sure all your flashlights are available and in working order. Use your battery-powered radio to see when the tornado watch will end or if it will escalate into a tornado warning. During a tornado warning, all staff and patrons should stay indoors. Everyone should be directed to a safe interior location for the duration of the storm. The ideal area should be the lowest level of the building, and it should be away from any doors. For additional protection, take cover under heavy furniture.[10] If a tornado occurs, do not evacuate the building. If possible, persons in the building should move to the lowest level, such as the lower stacks, staying away from windows, or to an inner hallway or small inner room away from windows. Taking cover under heavy furniture can provide additional protection. Because there is the possibility that the roof may collapse, it is advised to avoid seeking shelter in large hallways.

Recovery

If the library has suffered damage due to tornado, the operations coordinator should contact the library's insurance provider. The insurance provider's contact information, the policy number, and a copy of the policy should all be contained within the disaster plan. As discussed previously, when the tornado was declared a major disaster by the U.S. government, you should apply for FEMA aid to help you in the recovery process.

EARTHQUAKE

Damage Prevention

If your library is in an area that has a high risk of earthquakes, one of the best things you can do to prevent damage is to make sure all of your shelving is properly braced to the wall. If you have freestanding shelving, consider adding bungee cords across the front of books and other items on each shelf. If there is a minor earthquake, this would likely prevent the books from falling to the ground, but the small cord would not impede users from accessing the collection's book in day-to-day situations.

Response

When an earthquake happens, the building should not be evacuated. Persons in the building should stay in the inner core of the building away from windows. Shelter should be taken in a doorway; in a narrow corridor; or under a heavy table, desk, or bench. Also, be aware that aftershocks may follow for several hours or days after the earthquake. A battery-powered radio should be available so that instructions concerning the earthquake can be monitored.

Recovery

If your library has suffered any damage due to the earthquake have the operations coordinator contact your insurance provider right away to begin the claims process. As stated previously, when the earthquake has been given the designation of a major disaster, the operations coordinator should also apply for FEMA aid. Aftershocks will continue to happen for several weeks after major earthquakes, and some may be large enough to cause additional damage, so keep your guard up. The communications coordinator will need to make sure that the library staff are aware of any closures, and they should also be informed when services are up and running as normal.

This chapter has covered the best ways to prevent disasters from occurring, how to respond to a disaster when it occurs, and the most effective way to recover from a disaster. The next chapter will provide information about communication procedures during an emergency.

NOTES

1. Western Museums Association. Accessed January 18, 2018. http://www.westmuse.org/.
2. "CPR Facts and Stats." Accessed January 18, 2018. http://cpr.heart.org/AHAECC/CPRAndECC/AboutCPRFirstAid/CPRFactsAndStats/UCM_475748_CPR-Facts-and-Stats.jsp.
3. "Emergency Procedures Policy." Sibley Public Library. Accessed January 18, 2018. http://www.sibley.lib.ia.us/library-information/policies/emergencyprocedures/emergencyprocedurespolicy.
4. Dorn, Michael. "20 Active Shooter and Active Killer Prevention Strategies." *Campus Safety Magazine.* June 17, 2017. Accessed January 18, 2018. https://www.campussafetymagazine.com/news/20_active_shooter_and_active_killer_prevention_strategies/.
5. Kautzman, Amy, and Jennifer Little. "Active Shooter in the Library: How to Plan for, Prevent, and Survive the Worst." *Library Leadership and Management*, 25, no.1 (2011), 1–9.
6. Ibid.
7. Department of Homeland Security. Bomb Form. Accessed July 5, 2018. https://www.dhs.gov/publication/dhs-bomb-threat-checklist.
8. "DPlan™: The Online Disaster-Planning Tool." Accessed January 18, 2018. https://dplan.org.
9. "Federal Assistance in Severe Storms and Tornadoes: Our Role." FEMA.gov. Accessed January 18, 2018. https://www.fema.gov/blog/2011-04-07/federal-assistance-severe-storms-and-tornadoes-our-role.
10. "DPlan™: The Online Disaster-Planning Tool."

Date	
Time	
Location	

Name (Last, Middle, First)	
Date of Birth (MM/DD/YYYY)	
Phone Number	
Address	

Description of the Accident

Nature of Injury	
Body Area	

First Aid Refusal
I hereby refuse the first aid treatment recommended to me for the illness or injury incurred by me on this date. In signing this waiver, I release the [insert name of library here] and its staff from any liability resulting from this refusal to accept such first aid treatment.
Signature

Witness	Address	Phone Number

Name of Person Completing Report	Signature

Figure 3.1 Accident Report Form

QUESTIONS TO ASK CALLER		DATE	
WHEN IS THE BOMB GOING TO EXPLODE?		TIME CALL WAS RECEIVED	
		TIME CALL WAS ENDED	
WHERE IS THE BOMB LOCATED?		PHONE NUMBER WHERE CALL WAS RECEIVED	
WHAT DOES THE BOMB LOOK LIKE?			

WHAT KIND OF BOMB IS IT?

WHAT WILL CAUSE THE BOMB TO EXPLODE?

DID YOU PLACE THE BOMB? IF YES, WHY?

WHAT IS YOUR NAME?

CALLER'S VOICE		BACKGROUND NOISES	CALLER'S LANGUAGE
MALE	RASPY	ANIMAL NOISES	INCOHERENT
FEMALE	DEEP	STREET NOISES	READING
OLD	HIGH PITCH	VOICES	FROM A
YOUNG	CRACKED	MUSIC	SCRIPT
CALM	VOICE	STATIC	RECORDED
ANGRY	DISGUISED	HOUSE NOISES	MESSAGE
EXCITED	ACCENT	KITCHEN	IRRATIONAL
SLOW	DEEP	NOISES	PROFANE
SOFT	BREATHING	OFFICE	WELL SPOKEN
LOUD	RAPID	MACHINERY	
LAUGHTER	WHISPERED	FACTORY	
CRYING	FAMILIAR	MACHINERY	
NORMAL	SLURRED	PA SYSTEM	
DISTINCT	NASAL	CONVERSATION	
	STUTTER	MOTORS	
	LISP		

Figure 3.2 Bomb Threat Form

Source: Adapted from Department of Homeland Security Bomb Threat Checklist.

Use this pest trap log to help you keep track of any pest activity.

Date	Trap Number	Location	Checked By	Findings
The date when the trap was checked should be entered here.	List the trap number here.	Write the location of this trap within the building.	Have the person who checked the trap write their name down here.	List what the findings (if any) were in each trap.
11/30/2017	001	1st Floor Study Room	Jeff Duane	Empty
11/30/207	002	Periodicals	Jeff Duane	Silverfish

Figure 3.3 Pest Trap Log

CHAPTER 4

Communication Procedures

When a disaster occurs, everyone from the staff to the patrons to the general public will want to know what is going on. It is the library's job to communicate to everyone what is unfolding and what is being done about the situation in a clear and effective way. Putting together a communications plan is an easy way for you to have a structured guide to help you through the life cycle of a disaster. It will provide you with guidance on how to communicate before, during, and after a disaster to ensure that you eliminate or minimize any mistakes that might occur if you are not prepared with a plan. It is the responsibility of the communications coordinator to put together this plan. A good communications plan will help you minimize the risk of negative publicity for your library, and when handled correctly, it can even enhance your library's standing with the public.

BEFORE A DISASTER

Before a disaster occurs, use this time to gather the necessary information that you will need when a disaster occurs. The first item needed for your communications plan is the contact information for anyone you will need to communicate with during a disaster, including the disaster team leader, health and safety coordinator, and others. You will also need the contact information of those persons you need to give information to including the library director and the media. Basic contact information should include office phone numbers, cell phone numbers, fax numbers, and e-mail addresses for each person on your list. Make a physical copy and a digital copy of this contact information and keep it updated regularly. The communications plan should also have all the current methods of contact the library currently uses, who is responsible for each method, and how to reach each person. For example, if your library uses the home page of your website to report on any disasters or emergencies, the contact information of the person in charge of posting information to the website should be listed in your communication plan. This should also be updated regularly as job duties may not always remain the same. You will also want to gather some facts and statistics about your library. Reporters will need this information when reporting on the disaster, so make it easily available to them so that they do not incorrectly report information in haste. Limit this information to one page for quick dissemination, and make it simple and easy to read.

Next up on your to-do list is to decide who will be the library's spokesperson. Because part of the day-to-day tasks of the communications coordinator involve learning how to effectively communicate, this person usually takes on the role of spokesperson, but if there is good reason to assign this role to another person, someone else can also be the library's spokesperson. If the communications coordinator is not selected to be the library's spokesperson, then whoever is chosen should work closely with the communications coordinator before, during, and after a disaster.

Before a disaster occurs is the perfect time to establish a relationship with your local press and media. Is there someone in the library who sends out press releases when there are newsworthy stories occurring in your library? It is the communications coordinator's job to find out the recipients of these press releases and reach out to introduce yourself. Let them know what role you are playing within the library and how you can be of service. Ask them if they would like to receive the fact sheet that you have compiled for them to keep for reference, and promptly e-mail it to them. If you update the fact sheet, be sure to get them an updated copy as well. Use this time to conduct mock press conference exercises with the entire disaster team. See the mock press conference form (in Figure 4.2) for more information.

The communications coordinator should also work with the risk assessment coordinator to understand what disasters your institution is at highest risk for. See the risk assessment form (Figure 1.3 in Chapter 1) for more information. As you work together, see if there are ways for you to minimize risk, and go about trying to implement the ideas that are possible. If minimizing risk is not possible, then the communications coordinator needs to think about how to respond should any of these disasters occur and create a preplanned statement, which is also sometimes called a holding statement.

DURING A DISASTER

During a disaster, the communications coordinator will try to quickly gather as much information as possible to get a hold of the situation. You will want to know what happened, where in the library it happened, and when it occurred. Once you have that information, try to find out why the disaster or emergency happened and if anyone was affected by the incident. Finally, uncover what is being done to remediate the situation.

The communications coordinator is in charge of communicating messages to a variety of people based on the particular type of disaster occurring using all available communication tools. These messages should be sent to all library staff, and patrons should be given the option to opt-in to these messages as well. Examples of each of these types of messages are given at the end of this chapter. The communications coordinator will also need to be prepared for the different types of questions that will be asked during this situation. Staff may begin asking questions like:

- "When should I report to work?"
- "Will I get paid while the library is closed or can I collect unemployment?"
- "What happened to [coworker's name]?"
- "What are you going to do to address my safety?"
- "Is it safe to go back to work?"

While managers may ask questions like:

- "What happened?"
- "When did it happen?"
- "What damage did the library's building receive?"
- "What damage did the library's collection receive?"
- "How long will it be before the library will be up and running again?"

Patrons may also have questions like:

- "How will I return my books?"
- "Will you waive overdue fines until the library reopens?"
- "When will library programs resume?"

During this time, the director or the communications coordinator will also need to put out a statement immediately, so it may be helpful to have a holding statement already prepared, as previously mentioned. This is your preplanned general statement that you can release while you are gathering more facts. The holding statement should be sent to the media, staff, patrons, and any other relevant parties. It should state that:

- The library staff are aware of the situation. At this point, acknowledge what you know about the situation. What happened? Where did it happen? When did it happen? Who was involved? Why did it happen?
- More facts are being gathered. This will cover you for whatever facts you are currently unaware of.
- Actions are being taken. Only discuss what you are willing to make public at this moment.
- Staff members are concerned that the disaster has happened.
- On a specific day and time, an update will be given.

Make sure that your holding statement does not include any details that are unconfirmed or uncertain. Do not lay blame on anyone in your holding statement, and if the disaster has caused fatalities, do not list the names of victims at this time. To avoid confusion, be sure not to use acronyms or library jargon in your statement.

The statement should be posted through e-mail, text, media release, somewhere on the library's home page, and all social media accounts. Once you release the holding statement, it is your job to find out everything you can about the situation and deliver on your promise of an update. When sending your statement to the media, you may also want to send them the most updated fact sheet that you have compiled before the disaster occurred. Remember that the basic library information sheet should include information such as a brief history of the library; the library's mission statement; and some statistics such as the population that is served by the library, the number of cardholders the library has, annual circulation numbers, the number of staff members employed by the library, and the size and age of the building.

In addition to a written statement to the press, you may find yourself having to take part in a press conference where you will have to speak in person to reporters. When holding your press conference, make sure that the place chosen has a podium or desk and enough room for all the reporters who are present. The library's logo should appear behind the podium or desk, if possible. If not, a blank wall or screen is an appropriate alternative. Have microphones available, and assign someone with the proper technical skills to oversee that the equipment is installed correctly and can help with any technical difficulties during the press conference, should they occur. Have printed copies of your written statement and the library's fact sheet available to reporters. If the communications coordinator is not the library's spokesperson, then the communications coordinator should moderate the press conference and introduce the spokesperson. There should be no PowerPoint presentations or visual aids of any kind; the focus should be on the spokesperson's statement and in getting the reporter's questions answered. The spokesperson should begin by expressing sympathy to all those who were affected by the disaster. From there, follow the written statement as a guide, updating information wherever possible. Finally, open the floor to questions from reporters.

As reporters start asking questions, the spokesperson should be prepared to receive some difficult questions such as hostile questions, questions to which you do not have the answers, and off-topic questions. Hostile questions are becoming more common than in years past due to the aggressive nature of the 24-hour news cycle. These types of questions can be defined as questions with negative preconditions ("Is this going to be just like the last hurricane when the library was shut down for two months?") or questions that use hostile language ("Why is the recovery effort taking ridiculously long to complete?"). The best way to handle these types of questions is to avoid repeating the hostile language used in the question, reframe the question in less hostile or neutral terms, make the response short in length to avoid giving unnecessary fodder to the reporter, and make certain that the person answering the question does not mimic the same hostile tone received from the reporter when responding. In other words, remain calm, speak in a neutral tone, avoid repeating hostile words, and keep your statement short and to the point. For questions you do not have the answer, a simple "I don't know" can hurt your creditability, so it should be avoided. Instead, first acknowledge the value of the question, then be truthful and explain that you are going to need to look into it more. ("That is an excellent question, Ms. Garcia, we will need to look into that more before we can give you an appropriate answer.") Another option is to bookend the information you do not know with what you do know about the situation and how you are going to figure out the information you do not know. Let us suppose a reporter asks, "When will the library be opening again?" You can respond "I do know that we have quite a bit to work through before we can be fully operable. I do not know when we will be open again but I will speak with those directly involved in our recovery efforts to get an answer." Sometimes you may also find reporters asking questions that would be considered off-topic. In this situation, politely inform the reporter that the question is out of the scope of this press conference, and redirect the conversation back to your key message.

AFTER A DISASTER

After a disaster occurs but before the library is back to its day-to-day operations, the communications coordinator will need to remain in regular contact with staff, patrons, board members and/or administrators, and the press and media. Neglecting this duty will only allow for rumors to spread, and you may face the possibility of negative press. Once rumors and negative press occur, it can be nearly impossible to stop from spreading, so it is best to avoid them at all costs if possible. As progress is made, keep everyone informed. Once the library's day-to-day operations are back up and running, put together an evaluation of the situation and describe where you excelled and where you could use improvement. This evaluation will be part of a larger report organized by all the members of the disaster team. See Chapter 8, "After the Disaster Plan," for more information.

DISASTER NOTIFICATIONS EXAMPLES

Examples of each of these types of messages are given below in the context of the type of disaster. They vary because different emergencies have different possibilities.

Flooding

Text Message 1: [Insert library's name here] is currently experiencing flooding issues. Please avoid location until further notice.

Text Message 2: Flood Alert. The area surrounding [insert library's name here] is currently experiencing flooding issues. Please avoid location until further notice.

E-mail/Voicemail 1: This is [insert library's name here] with a flood alert. The [insert library's name here] is currently flooding. Please avoid location until further notice.

E-mail/Voicemail 2: This is [insert library's name here] with a flood alert. The area surrounding [insert library's name here] is currently flooding. If you are in the area, seek higher ground immediately. If you are at home or in the library, stay where you are. For additional information and updates, go to [state where they can go to find updates, i.e., the library's website or social media page].

Fire

Text Message: There is a fire at [insert library's name here]. Evacuate if you are in the building. If you are not in the area, stay clear of the area.

E-mail/Voicemail: This is [insert library's name here] with a fire alert. A fire has been reported at [insert library's name here]. If you are in the building, evacuate immediately. If you are not in the area, stay clear so that emergency units and firefighters can work unobstructed. For additional information and updates, go to [state where they can go to find updates].

Wildfire

Text Message: Wildfire Alert: There is a fast-moving wildfire near [insert library's name here]. If you are in the building, evacuate immediately and head toward [list evacuation location here].

E-mail/Voicemail: This is [insert library's name here] with a wildfire alert. There is a fast-moving wildfire near [insert library's name here]. Evacuations have been ordered. If you are in the library, evacuate immediately toward [list evacuation location here]. If you are not in the area, stay away. For additional information and updates, go to [state where they can go to find updates].

Active Shooter

Text Message: [Insert library name] is issuing an active shooter alert. A suspect with a weapon is on the premises. Go into the nearest room and lock the door. Follow instructions from authorities.

E-mail/Voicemail: [Insert library name] is issuing an active shooter alert. There is a suspect with a [type] weapon on the premises. If you are in the library, go into the nearest available room and lock the door. If you are not in the library, stay away. THIS IS NOT A TEST. Wait for the all clear notification from local authorities. For additional information and updates, go to [state where they can go to find updates].

Bomb Threat

Text Message: [Insert library name] is issuing bomb threat alert. [Insert library's name here] has received a bomb threat. If you are in the building, evacuate immediately. Follow instructions from authorities.

E-mail/Voicemail: [Insert library's name here] is issuing bomb threat alert. A bomb threat has been received by [insert library's name here]. If you are near the library, prepare immediately for possible evacuation. Listen for instructions from local authorities and follow them quickly and carefully. For additional information and updates, go to [state where they can go to find updates].

Bomb Found

Text Message: [Insert library name] is issuing bomb alert. A bomb has been found the library. Prepare to evacuate. Follow instructions from authorities.

E-mail/Voicemail: [Insert library name] is issuing bomb alert. A bomb has been found in the library. Avoid the vicinity of the library. If you are not in the area, stay away. If you are near the library, prepare immediately for possible evacuation. Listen for instructions from local authorities, and follow them quickly and carefully. For additional information and updates, go to [state where they can go to find updates].

Tornado

Text Message: [Insert library's name here] Alert: A tornado warning has been issued for [insert library's name here]. Visit [emergency website] for more details.

E-mail/Voicemail 1: [Insert library's name here] Alert: A tornado warning has been issued for the [insert library's name here]. A tornado warning means that a tornado has been sighted on the ground and you should take immediate action to take cover. Stay away from windows, doors, and walls that face the building's exterior.

- Go to a shelter area, such as a basement or the lowest level in the building.
- If there is no basement, go to the center of an interior room on the lowest level (closet, interior hallway) away from corners, windows, doors, and outside walls.
- Put as many walls as possible between you and the outside.
- Get under a sturdy table and use your arms to protect your head and neck.
- Do not open the windows.
- If a tornado hits and you sustain injuries, or witness others being injured, call 911.
- If the tornado warning is extended or lifted, an update will be posted at [state where they can go to find updates].

E-mail/Voicemail: This is an alert emergency message for the [insert library's name here]. A tornado warning has been issued until [time] today. A tornado warning means that a tornado has been sighted on the ground and you should take immediate action to take cover. For additional information and updates, go to [state where they can go to find updates].

Earthquake

Text Message: [Insert library's name here] Alert: An earthquake has occurred. Do not evacuate. You should remain in the library until further notice.

E-mail/Voicemail 2: Earthquake Alert: An earthquake has just occurred. For your safety, do not evacuate the library. Remain inside until further information. We will provide updates as we receive more information. For additional information and updates, go to [state where they can go to find updates].

All Clear

Text Message/E-mail/Voicemail: The [specify the type of emergency] emergency has ended. Please stand by for further instructions. Go to [state where they can go to find updates] for more information.

By detailing what goes into a communications plan and providing sample scripts to use during a disaster, this chapter has helped you put together an effective plan for communication. The next chapter will focus on salvage procedures your library will need to utilize during the recovery of a disaster.

Communications Coordinator Name
Communications Coordinator Job Title
Communications Coordinator Phone Number
Communications Coordinator E-mail Address

Date: DD/MM/YYYY
Time: HH:MM

[Library name] can confirm that at [insert day and time] a [insert type of disaster] occurred.

At this time, we have established that [insert known facts about the disaster here]. The library is [insert what actions are currently taking place to address the disaster].

The library would like to [insert an expression of concern and/or sympathy for what has happened].

More facts are currently being gathered, and we will provide an update at [insert day and time]. Updates will be provided by [list method(s) of delivery i.e., website, social media, press conference, etc.].

Figure 4.1   Library Holding Statement Template

Instructions: *The disaster team will help the communications coordinator and library spokesperson prepare for a press conference. The disaster team will play the role of the reporters, while the library spokesperson and/or communications coordinator will answer the questions and/or moderate the questions. The mock press conference exercise should be completed at least twice a year.*

Roles

Reporters: Reporters will prepare questions to ask during the press conference. If the who, what, when, where, and why questions have not been covered by the library's previous written statement, make certain to ask those questions. Also be sure to include hostile questions and off-topic questions.

Spokesperson and Moderator: Prepare your key message. Use the written press release statement as a guide. If you have received updated information since you created the written press statement, make sure the update information is included in your key message. Answer the questions as best as you can, be sympathetic, honest, and avoid speculation. Avoid falling into any traps set up by reporters. Remain calm at all times. If your promise to follow up on information, do not forget to follow through with your promise.

Disaster Scenarios

Scenario #1: A major hurricane hit the area surrounding the library yesterday evening. The storm has passed and the staff members who arrived this morning at 7 A.M. discover 4 inches of water in the basement, which holds the library's children's collection. There appears to be significant damage to all of the books on the lower shelves. On the second floor, a window appears to have broken due to the hurricane. The communications coordinator prepares a statement, which includes the following information:

- A flood occurred in the basement of the library.
- Damage has been caused to parts of the collection and parts of the building.
- The library will remain closed until further notice.

The communications coordinator has informed the local media that they will be having a press conference at 12 noon in the lobby of the library to discuss the hurricane damage.
Other Relevant Info:

- A hurricane hit the library two years ago and water flooded the basement, and the library was not fully operational until two months after the incident.

Scenario #2: Around 3 P.M., a bomb threat was called in to the library. Bomb threat procedures were followed, and the library was evacuated. Emergency responders arrived on the scene, and after it was discovered that there was no bomb, the emergency responders gave the all clear to reenter the building. Before the all clear was given, the streets surrounding the library were blocked off for anyone except emergency vehicles. Because this was during rush hour, it has caused quite a stir in the area alerting the press and local media who have been calling the library. The communications coordinator put out a written statement, which includes the following information:

- At approximately 3 P.M. this afternoon, a bomb threat was called into the library.
- The library was immediately evacuated.
- Emergency responders arrived and determined that there was no bomb present and gave the all clear for everyone to return to the library.

Figure 4.2 Mock Press Conference Form

The press statement is not satisfactory for the local media; they want to interview someone at the library so that they can air a story about the incident for the 11 P.M. news. The communications coordinator has informed the local press and media that a press conference will be held at 8 P.M. that evening in the lobby of the library.

Other relevant info:

- In the library's 20-year history, there has never been a bomb threat received before.

Scenario #3: At approximately 12 noon an armed individual came into the library and shot another person. Active shooter procedures were followed by the library staff, and law enforcement and emergency responders arrived on the scene a short while later. Law enforcement was able to apprehend the shooter, and the victim was taken to the hospital. The communications coordinator put out a written statement, which includes the following information:

- At approximately 12 noon this afternoon, an armed individual came into the library and shot another person. (No names are mentioned.)
- Law enforcement was able to apprehend the shooter, and the victim was taken to the hospital. The victim's condition is unknown at this point.
- The library has been closed for the day and will not reopen until further notice.

The communications coordinator has informed the press and media that a press conference will be held outside the library at 6 P.M. this evening.

Other Relevant Info:

- At 4 P.M., law enforcement informs the library that they will need at least 24–48 hours to go through the crime scene to collect evidence.
- At 5 P.M., the library is informed that the victim is in critical condition.
- Six weeks ago, a minor in the library was found with a gun in his backpack. Authorities were called, and no one was hurt.

Create Your Own Scenario:

After using the examples listed above, feel free to create your own scenarios for your mock press conference exercises. Use the template below to guide you:

Scenario	Choose a disaster. Use disasters most likely to affect your library, and if you have time, use disasters less likely to occur.
	Choose a time of day. Practice scenarios that occur at different times of day. Remember that television reporters will want to have news for the morning, early evening, and late evening new airings.
	Decide what has been damaged and who (if any) has been injured. Is there damage to the collection? If so, what?
	Is there damage to the building? If so, where?
	Have any staff or patrons been injured? If so, how many?

Figure 4.2   (*Continued*)

Written Statement	Based on the scenario information, the communications coordinator should put together a mock written statement for everyone to view.
Other Relevant Info	Any updates from the time the press release was written until the press conference is held should be listed here. Any previous incidents should be listed here.

After each exercise, the documentation coordinator should write a report consisting of the communications coordinator's self-evaluation and the disaster team leader's evaluation of how the communications coordinator performed and areas where they could improve. The report can help the communications coordinator to be ready for the next time this exercise is undertaken.

Figure 4.2   (*Continued*)

CHAPTER 5

Salvage Procedures

If your collection is damaged in a disaster, it is most likely to have water damage, mold damage, fire and smoke damage, and pest damage. This chapter will help you to salvage your collection from these types of damages. It will also discuss the supplies needed; how to prepare, pack, and handle your items; and the preferred method for getting them in their best shape. This chapter will also inform you on how to know when an item is not salvageable and should be replaced instead.

SALVAGING WATER-DAMAGED MATERIALS

Salvaging water-damaged materials can require a lot of work. There are various methods for salvaging, all dependent on an assortment of factors, the two biggest factors being the type of water damage and the type of object.

Types of Water Damage

Objects that suffer from minor water damage are the easiest to salvage. Examples of minor water-related disasters include small roof or plumbing leaks. In this case, the materials affected are usually a small quantity and can be easily air-dried or frozen. Success rates are highest in these scenarios because you can focus on the materials since utilities are not usually affected and remain operational and so day-to-day operations are not affected. For this type of damage, you can call on your salvage coordinator to complete the salvage process; there is generally no need to seek outside help. In addition, all the resources you need should already be stocked in your emergency supply kits, so the costs are relatively minimal.

Objects that suffer from moderate water damage will be more challenging to salvage, but success is still achievable in these situations. Examples of moderate water damage include burst water pipes or a sewer backup. The main challenge with moderate water damage is that you will have to balance salvaging your materials with getting your library back on track, as it is highly likely that regular day-to-day operations have been disrupted after a moderate water-related disaster. You may also find yourself needing to order more supplies than you have on hand, and you may need to seek out a conservator or preservationist for the proper salvage of some items.

You will face your biggest challenge when major water damage affects your library's materials. Examples of major water-related disasters include floods and hurricanes. In these situations, your utilities will most likely be out of order, your day-to-day operations have been completely disrupted, and due to safety reasons, you may not have access to your collection. Because time is of the essence when it comes to salvaging, lack of access will be the biggest challenge to successful salvaging. If you experience a delay of more than 48 hours to accessing your collection, you may also find yourself dealing with a mold outbreak.

Basic Salvage Procedures

The process for salvaging wet materials will look something like this:

Step 1: Gathering Supplies. You will need different supplies for different objects. Gather up the items listed under each object in the following section.

Step 2: Packing and Handling. You will most likely be moving the wet materials to a designated salvage area where you can control both the temperature and relative humidity. It is important that you don't do any added damage to the materials when you pack them to take to the salvage area, so you will need to understand the proper way to pack and handle the objects.

Step 3: Preparing the Objects for Salvage. Before you can dry the items, you must prepare each object.

Step 4: Drying. The preferred method of drying will depend on the type of object you are attempting to dry.

Various Drying Methods

Vacuum Freeze-Drying

Vacuum freeze-drying works by placing frozen materials in a vacuum chamber. The vacuum is pulled, a source of heat is introduced, and the collections that are dried at temperatures below 32 F remain frozen. The water sublimates directly from a solid (ice) state to a gaseous (vapor) state. The ice or solvent crystals are removed without melting. Because of the way this process works, there is no additional wetting, swelling, or distortion of the items beyond that incurred before the frozen materials were placed in the chamber. If this process is used on wet materials quickly after the water damage is incurred, then very little extra shelf or storage space will be required when they are dry. Ten percent additional shelf space is a sound estimate to use for planning.[1]

Coated papers come with their own set of challenges, since it can be difficult to dry if there is any blocking. Blocking occurs when the wet pages of a book stick together when drying. Because of this, all coated papers should be frozen at 10 F or lower within six hours of water damage. They may then be vacuum freeze-dried.[2] Vacuum freeze-drying can be used on rare and unique materials, but this process should be avoided on leathers and vellums, as they may not survive.[3]

The main pro of vacuum freeze-drying is that it is the most effective method of drying. Your success rate will be greatest using this process. Vacuum freeze-drying is also suitable for a large amount of items, and it can be used on coated papers as well. It should also be mentioned that there are a few cons to using vacuum freeze-drying. This process is quite expensive, especially if you have only a small amount of items that need to undergo this type of drying. In addition, this is not something that you can easily do in-house; a professional service that does vacuum freeze-drying must be called, and there aren't a lot of companies to choose from. This may be problematic if you are located in a rural area and there is no one offering this service near you. You also may run into problems if the cause of the water damage is a community-effected disaster (e.g., hurricane and flood), since these services will be in high demand and you might have to wait for availability. Then, there is also the issue of books coming out of this process very dry (sometimes overly dry) because there is no humidity in a vacuum. For very valuable books, always check with a conservator before choosing a drying method.

Vacuum Thermal Drying

Vacuum thermal drying is similar to vacuum freeze-drying as materials are put into a vacuum chamber to be dried. The main difference is that while the vacuum freeze-drying process goes from a solid state to a gaseous state, skipping the liquid state, vacuum thermal drying does not skip the liquid state; it goes from the solid state through the liquid state to the gaseous state. What this means for the materials is that you will notice your items, while dry, will have serious distortion, and many items will most likely need to be flattened or will need rebinding. It will also cause the blocking of coated paper and does not work for leather vellum, some photographs, and microforms. On the plus side, it is a good drying method for materials that have no long-term value, and it is suitable for a large amount of items.[4]

Dehumidification

The dehumidification process works by using large commercial dehumidifiers to stabilize the environment. They are placed in a facility with all the collections, equipment, and furnishings left in place. Dry air is then introduced at a very low humidity level of less than 15 percent, and the temperature will reach anywhere from 79 to 99 F. One of the biggest pros of the dehumidification process is that you do not need to remove your water-damaged items from the shelves; they remain in place while the dehumidifiers work. This is also beneficial if you have a large amount of items, as moving them to a salvage area will take up a great deal of time. The process is also relatively fast, taking only a couple of days. Your materials also remain on site and accessible as opposed to other methods where your items are taken to the service provider's facility. This is also a good drying method if there has been extensive water damage to the building structure since it will help dry not only the collection but also the physical area that the dehumidifiers are located in. There are cons to using this drying method, the main one being that dehumidification is successful only on damp materials; very wet materials will need to use an alternate drying method. This method is also not suitable for coated papers or any items that have water-soluble inks or pigments.[5]

Thermaline or Cryogenic Drying

This drying method utilizes a more advanced variation of freeze-drying. The best thing about this drying process is that there is no distortion and you can use it for leather-bound books and vellum. However, the biggest con of this drying process is that out of all the methods listed here, it is the most expensive due to the individual handling provided for every item. Because of this, this method is primarily used for rare book and manuscript collections.[6]

Freeze-Drying

This method of drying involves using a self-defrosting blast freezer to dry the items. During this process, the freezer is set to a temperature between 10 and 40 F, and wet materials placed in the freezer should dry anywhere from several weeks to several months. The biggest con of this method is that it takes a very long amount of time. To circumvent this issue, it is usually used in conjunction with the air-drying method. Another con of freeze-drying is that very wet materials will not be able to sufficiently dry with this method. Very wet materials should use the vacuum freeze-drying method or should use the freeze-drying method with the air-drying method. Coated papers must be interleaved with wax paper when using this method, or the risk of blocking may occur.

Air-Drying

The air-drying method involves drying materials under normal indoor environmental conditions, generally at a temperature of 70 to 75°F and a relative humidity of 40 to 55 percent. It is the most frequently used method of drying wet items, although not always the most effective. The biggest pro of air-drying is that it is the lowest cost of all the drying methods and it can be done by yourself. Combined with freeze-drying, air-drying can be done in batches so that you have more time to get things done. However, this method does require a lot of physical space for drying, and the drying process can be very time-consuming. Finally, even when you follow all the drying instructions to a T, you will still see various levels of distortion for most paper-based objects.

Cloth-Bound Books

Supplies Needed

- Bread tray (to rinse dirty books)
- Paper towels or blotting paper (for absorbing water)
- Plastic sheeting (for covering tables)
- Bricks (for flattening items)
- PVA sponge (A synthetic sponge essentially composed of polyvinyl alcohol. It has impressive retention and wicking properties. PVA sponge will absorb up to 12 times its dry weight in water.)
- Dehumidifier (to keep the humidity at suggested levels)
- Fans (to keep air circulating)
- Milk crates (for packing)
- Cardboard boxes and plastic bags (alternative to milk crates)
- Scissors (for cutting blotter paper)

Packing and Handling

Cloth-bound books should be packed spine down in milk crates. Milk crates are great packing containers because the holes in the crates allow for air circulation, but cardboard boxes lined with plastic bags can be used if milk crates are unavailable. When handling these books, do not open or close them or separate covers when packing and make certain that any oversized books are fully supported.

Preparing for Salvage

Once you have moved your cloth-bound books to the designated salvage area, you will need to rinse any books that have mud or dirt on them. On a table, place a bread tray with clean water in it. If you have multiple people working on this, give everyone his or her own bread tray to expedite this process. Take one book at a time, and carefully swish the closed book through the tray to clean off any dirt and debris. Place the book aside, and continue until all your books are free from any mud, dirt, or debris. Remember to periodically change out the dirty water for fresh water as needed. Leave out whatever amount of books you think you can salvage in 48 hours in the salvage area to begin drying, and place the rest of the books in a freezer to salvage at a later time.

Preferred Drying Method

For cloth-bound books, the preferred drying method is vacuum freeze-drying, freeze-drying, or air-drying.

How to Air-Dry Cloth-Bound Books

If your cloth-bound book is extremely wet:
Do not open extremely wet books, since the wet paper is extremely delicate and will tear easily. Instead, stand the book up and place it on top of blotting paper or paper towels and place a small PVA sponge under the fore edge of the book to allow water to drain from the book more efficiently. You may have to cut your PVA sponge for a better fit. If the book cannot stand alone, then support it with nonmetal bookends or blocks of wood. Replace the paper when it becomes damp, usually every 20 to 30 minutes. Continue this process until water is no longer dripping. Follow the instructions for moderately wet books.

If your cloth-bound book is moderately wet:
Cut blotting paper or paper towels to be slightly bigger than the size of the pages of the book (this helps to accelerate absorption). Then lay the book on its side and insert blotting paper or paper towels every 30 pages or so (if you insert too many pieces of paper, you run the risk of distorting the book). Replace the absorbent paper when it becomes damp (every 20–30 minutes). Each time you replace the paper towels, turn the book over on the other side to minimize distortion. Continue this process until the book is damp. Follow the instructions for damp books.

If your cloth-bound book is damp:
Place books on their fore edge and fan out the pages. Turn your electric fan on but do not allow it to flap the pages of the book; wet books have the possibility of having mold on them. A fan that blows onto the books can allow mold to travel causing a mold outbreak. Let the book stand until it is thoroughly dry. This may take several days to a week to happen. Finally, place the dry book under a clean brick covered with cloth or paper) to reduce the rippling of pages.

Paperbacks

Supplies Needed

- Bread tray (to rinse dirty books)
- Paper towels or blotting paper (for absorbing water)
- Plastic sheeting (for covering tables)
- Bricks (for flattening items)
- PVA sponge (for absorbing water)
- Dehumidifier (to keep the humidity at suggested levels)
- Fans (to keep air circulating)
- Milk crates (for packing)
- Cardboard boxes and plastic bags (alternative to milk crates)
- Scissors (for cutting blotter paper)
- Fishing line (for drying)

Packing and Handling

Paperbacks should be packed spine down in milk crates. Cardboard boxes lined with plastic bags can be used if milk crates are unavailable. When handling these books, do not open or close them or separate covers when packing.

Preparing for Salvage

Once you have moved your paperbacks to the designated salvage area, you will need to rinse any books that have mud or dirt on them. On a table, place a bread tray with clean water in it. If you have multiple people working on this, give everyone his or her own bread tray to expedite this process. Take one book at a time, and carefully swish the closed book through the tray to clean off any dirt and debris. Place the paperback aside, and continue until all your books are free from any mud, dirt, or debris. Remember to periodically change out the dirty water for fresh water as needed. Leave out whatever amount of paperbacks you think you can salvage in 48 hours in the salvage area to begin drying, and place the rest of the books in a freezer to salvage at a later time.

Preferred Drying Method

For paperback books, the preferred drying method is vacuum freeze-drying, freeze-drying, or air-drying.

How to Air-Dry Paperback Books

If your paperback is extremely wet:
Lay the paperback flat on blotter paper or paper towels. Replace the absorbent paper every 20 to 30 minutes or whenever the paper is fully saturated, whichever comes first. Continue this process until the paperback is no longer dripping. Follow the instructions for moderately wet paperbacks.

If your paperback is moderately wet:

Interleave the paperback with blotting paper every 30 pages or so. Be careful that you don't interleave too much and cause damage to the spine. Replace these papers every 30 minutes or whenever the paper is fully saturated, whichever comes first. As you replace the blotting paper, flip the book to the other side so that distortion can be minimized. Continue this process until the book is damp. Follow the instructions for damp paperbacks.

If your paperback is damp:

Ideally, you will put your book on its fore edge and fan it out, though this is not always possible with a paperback. The alternative method here is to use fishing line to hang your paperbacks instead. Take some fishing line and tie it to two secure objects, just like a clothesline. Then, open the book to the center, and hang the paperback over the fishing line. Make sure to purchase fishing line that is strong enough (weight capability is usually listed on the package), and create lots of small hanging lines versus one long line. Turn on the electric fan, and leave paperbacks on the fishing line until they are dry. After they have dried, use bricks to weigh down the paperbacks to minimize distortion.

Leather-Bound Books

Supplies Needed

- Bread trays (to rinse dirty books)
- Blotter paper (for interleaving)
- Scissors (for cutting paper)
- Milk crates (for packing)
- Cardboard boxes and plastic bags (alternative to milk crates)
- Plastic sheeting (for covering tables)

Packing and Handling

Leather-bound books should be packed spine down in milk crates. Cardboard boxes lined with plastic bags can be used if milk crates are unavailable. When handling these books, do not open or close them or separate covers when packing, and make certain that any oversized books are fully supported.

Preparing for Salvage

Once you have moved your leather-bound books to the designated salvage area, you will need to rinse any books that have mud or dirt on them. On a table, place a bread tray with clean water in it. If you have multiple people working on this, give everyone his or her own bread tray to expedite this process. Take one book at a time, and carefully swish the closed book through the tray to clean off any dirt and debris. Place the book aside, and continue until all your books are free from any mud, dirt, or debris. Remember to periodically change out the dirty water for fresh water as needed. Leave out whatever amount of books you think you can salvage in 48 hours in the salvage area to begin drying, and place the rest of the books in a freezer to salvage at a later time.

Preferred Drying Method

For leather-bound books, the preferred method of drying is Thermaline or cryogenic drying. If that is not possible, air-drying is an acceptable method. Follow the instructions from cloth-bound books to dry these items.

Books with Coated Papers

If your library has a large collection of art or photography books, you will notice these types of books have a lot of coated pages.

Supplies Needed

- Bread trays (to rinse dirty books)
- Silicone-release paper (for interleaving)
- Wax paper (alternative to silicone-release paper)
- Scissors (for cutting paper)
- Plastic sheeting (for covering tables)
- Garbage cans and plastic bags (for prepping)

Packing and Handling

Within six hours of water damage, books with coated papers should be either frozen or placed in cold water to prevent blocking. If you can prevent blocking, then air-drying is usually successful in salvaging, though there will most likely be signs of cockling.

Preparing for Salvage

Because of their fragile nature, coated paper books should remain in clean cold water until they can be dealt with. This is because once they start to dry, the paper will block, and then you will not be able to salvage these items. Use a garbage can with a plastic bag inside to hold the cold water, and place the coated paper books in the water as soon as possible. As you prepare to salvage, remove each book one at a time, swish it through the bread tray to make sure it is clean, and then set aside. Remember to periodically change out the dirty water for fresh water as needed. Leave out whatever amount of books you think you can salvage in 48 hours in the salvage area to begin drying, and place the rest of the books in a freezer to salvage at a later time.

Preferred Drying Method

For books with coated paper, the preferred drying method is vacuum freeze-drying, freeze-drying, or air-drying.

How to Air-Dry Books with Coated Paper

Follow the instructions on how to air-dry cloth-bound books, except interleave any coated pages with silicone release paper or wax paper. These items should be checked regularly to make sure pages are not sticking together.

Photographs

A photograph is made up of a binder, image, and support. Over the years, the method for creating photographs has changed, and the material used to create the support has changed with it. The earliest supports were made of paper (salted paper prints) or metal (daguerreotypes). Experimentation led to a wide variety of supports including iron (tintypes), glass (ambrotypes), and paper (many different processes). In order to properly salvage a photograph, we need to know its composition. For salvaging purposes, we will organize photographs into three types:

1. Cased photographs
2. Photographic prints
3. Photographic negatives and positives on glass

Cased photographs like ambrotypes, daguerreotypes, tintypes, and glass plate negatives are the most vulnerable types of photographs and should take precedence over others. You should attempt to salvage these within 24 hours of water damage. Photographic prints like albumen prints, salter paper prints, and silver gelatin prints are less fragile, but you should attempt to salvage these within 48 hours.

Supplies Needed

- Blotter paper (for absorbing water)
- Plastic garbage bin with plastic bags (for prepping photos)
- Plastic trays (for rinsing prints)
- Clothesline (for air-drying prints)
- Clothes pins (for air-drying prints)

Packing and Handling

With any type of photograph, you should not touch the emulsion. To properly handle photographs, hold the photograph by the edge or margins. When laying a photograph down, it should always be placed with the emulsion side up. Any type of photograph that is wet will be extremely fragile, so be sure to handle with care.

Cased photographs and photographic negatives and positives on glass should be packed horizontally in a padded container. Photographic prints should be placed in garbage containers lined with plastic bags and should be immersed in cold water until you are ready to begin the drying process. Use different garbage containers for each type of photograph. If you foresee that you will not be able to dry all of your ambrotypes, daguerreotypes, tintypes, and glass plate negatives within 24 hours and all of your albumen prints, salter paper prints, and silver gelatin prints within 48 hours, contact a conservator for advice on whether it is safe to freeze these items.

Preparing for Salvage

Black and white prints can be cleaned by placing them one at a time in a bread tray filled with cool, clean water and swishing back and forth to remove any dirt and debris. Cased photographs should not be washed or removed from their cases. Photographs with glass supports should not be washed either; if these items have dirt or debris on them, contact a conservator to handle them.

Preferred Drying Method

For most photographs, the preferred method of drying is air-drying. Cased photographs and glass photographs should be placed on blotter papers with the photograph face up. Photographic prints can also be placed on blotter papers with the emulsion side up. They can also be hung on a clothesline to dry. You can use a clothesline or fishing line with clothes pins to hang the photographs up. Turn on the electric fan and turn on the portable dehumidifier if the relative humidity is too high in the salvage area.

Textiles and Clothing

Supplies Needed

- Terry cloth toweling (for blotting)
- PVA sponges (for absorbing water)
- Dehumidifier (for keeping humidity at recommended levels)
- Electric fan (to keep air circulating)
- Acid-free tissue (to aid in drying)
- Plastic sheeting (for protecting materials)
- Muslin fabric (for carrying materials)
- Large wooden boards (for carrying materials)

Packing and Handling

Remove any hanging clothing or textiles from their hangers, and use a sling made of muslin or similar fabric to support them as you transfer them to the salvage area. You can also use large wooden boards to transport your items, though they are heavier and bulkier than fabric slings. If you have a table that has wheels, you may want to use this to transport your items to the salvage area. Make sure you have at least two people lifting the items, as clothing and textiles can become extremely heavy when wet. If you have any materials that are folded, do not unfold them, transport them as is. When transporting items, do not stack materials on top of another, move them one at a time.

Preparing for Salvage

You will need to prepare a large workspace, as clothing and textiles cannot be placed on top of each other. You should have some folding tables with your emergency supply kits, but if you do not have enough, the floor can be used as an alternative space as well. Be sure to place plastic sheeting over the folding tables or the floor to protect the materials.

Preferred Drying Method

For clothing and textiles, the preferred method of drying is air-drying.

How to Air-Dry Clothing and Textiles

Extremely wet clothing or textiles will need to be blotted with PVA sponges and then have terry cloth toweling placed on top to get the excess water out. As the terry cloth toweling get saturated, replace with a dry piece of toweling. Continue this process until the item is somewhat dry. At this point, you may now unfold the garment or textile if needed. Lay the item flat and let air-dry. For items such as historical clothing or costumes, acid-free tissue should be placed in the garment to prevent creasing.

Painting, Prints, and Drawings

Supplies Needed

- Blotter paper
- Newsprint
- Bubble wrap
- Stretcher

Packing and Handling

When packing paintings, pad the corners of the frame or painting with bubble wrap and move the paintings vertically. Stand items upright with bubble wrap between paintings so that painted surfaces do not touch a rough surface. Oversized prints and drawings should be packed in map drawers, bread trays, flat boxes, or on heavy cardboard or poly-covered plywood. Anything that is flat and durable can be used to transport these items.

Preparing for Salvage

If there are any objects that are in frames, they should be removed from them to prepare for the drying process. If this task proves to be too difficult or if there is fear that the frame removal will cause further damage, then a conservator should be called in to help.

Preferred Drying Method

If your paintings, prints, or drawings are damp, then the preferred drying method is to freeze-dry or air-dry. If these objects are very wet, then freeze-drying is preferred.

How to Air-Dry Paintings

On your workspace, prepare a horizontal bed of blotter paper and unused newsprint, equal in thickness to the paint layer. If there is a backing, it should be removed to expose the wet canvas. Use blotter paper to absorb the water, and replace the blotter paper as it becomes saturated. Continue to do this until the painting is dry.

Wood Furniture

Supplies Needed

- Blotting materials
- Polyethylene sheeting
- Soft bristle brush

Packing and Handling

Lift from the bottom of the object for the best support. Extremely wet unpainted wooden objects should be wrapped with blotting materials, then wrapped in polyethylene sheeting to retain as much moisture as possible, since fast drying will cause irreversible damage.

Preparing for Salvage

Rinse or sponge clean the furniture with clear water to remove mud or dirt before drying. Be careful not to wipe too hard and damage the furniture's finish. Use a soft bristle brush to clean carvings and crevices. If mud or dirt has dried on the item, dampen the area with a sponge, and attempt to remove the mud or dirt with a wooden spatula.

Preferred Drying Method

For wood furniture, the preferred method of drying is air-drying.

How to Air-Dry Wood Furniture

Absorb excess moisture with sponges and clean towels. Blot, do not wipe, to avoid scratching the surface. Air-dry using fans to keep air moving without blowing directly on the pieces. Tent the objects with polyethylene sheeting to slow the drying. If possible, lift the items off the floor and place on a piece of lumber to allow air to circulate on all sides. Open any doors or drawers slightly to allow air to circulate inside the items. Use a dehumidifier to slowly remove moisture from the area and objects. Drying quickly will cause warping and cracking. Bring relative humidity down to 50 to 55 percent.

Microfiche and Film

Supplies Needed

- Clothes line (for drying)
- Clothes pins (for drying)
- Garbage bins with plastic bags (for prepping)
- Boxes lined in plastic (alternative to garbage bins)

Packing and Handling

Wipe the outside of film cans or boxes before opening. Cans that are wet on the outside may contain dry film that should be separated from wet material. If the fiche cannot be air-dried immediately, keep them wet inside a garbage bin or box lined with plastic bags until they can be dried.

Preferred Drying Method

Air-drying is the preferred drying method for microfiche. Remove the paper jackets from the microfiche to dry, but do not throw them out; they should be saved to preserve any information printed on them. Put this information onto new jackets once the fiche is dry and ready to be stored again. The best air-drying method is to clip the fiche to clotheslines with rust-proof clips. Fiche can be successfully vacuum freeze-dried, and if you are dealing with large quantities of fiche, this option should be investigated. Make sure that the vendor you choose has experience vacuum freeze-drying.

Vinyl Discs

Supplies Needed

- Padded plastic crates
- Distilled water
- Grease pencil
- Dish rack (for drying)

Packing and Handling

The safest way to handle any disc is to hold it by the edges. Pack these items vertically in padded plastic crates.

Preparing for Salvage

Remove all the discs from their sleeves and jackets. If there is mud or dirt on the discs, rinse in a container of distilled water. If the labels have separated, mark the center of the disc with a grease pencil and keep track of the label. Separate your vinyl discs by size.

Preferred Drying Method

The preferred drying method for vinyl discs is air-drying discs vertically on a rack.

CDs, DVDs, and USB Flash Drives

Supplies Needed for CDs and DVDs

- Distilled water
- Lint-free cotton cloth
- Wax paper
- CD/DVD rack (This will be used for drying.)

Supplies Needed for USB Flash Drives

- Uncooked rice
- Small flat screwdriver
- Sealable plastic bag

Packing and Handling

CDs and DVDs should be packed upright. When handling these discs, you should hold them by the outer edge. You can also hold your hand in the shape of an "L" and stick your pointer finger through the hole while your thumb holds the outer edge.

Preparing for Salvage

To prepare these items for drying, you will need to remove all CDs and DVDs from their cases and open the cases of the USB flash drives.

Preferred Drying Method

The preferred drying method for CDs and DVDs is to have them air-dried on a rack. USB flash drives should be air-dried as well. The case of the flash drive should be opened to allow moisture to evaporate and eliminate any possible corrosion. Use a small flat-blade screwdriver to separate the two halves of the case. Afterward, place some uncooked rice into a small plastic sealable bag, and then place the flash drive into the bag and seal the bag. The bag should be stored in an area with a relative humidity of 50 percent or lower for at least 24 hours. After 24 hours, examine the drive to see if any moisture is still present. If you can see any moisture, leave the drive in the plastic bag for 24 hours and repeat until the drive is completely dry. Finally, you can reassemble the case, making sure the two halves are tight shut. The flash drive should now be in working order.

SALVAGING MOLD-INFESTED MATERIALS

Removing Mold: Preparing for Salvage

Only after you have determined that no highly toxic species are present, you may begin to attempt to remove mold. The following protective gear and procedures are necessary for safely dealing with minor outbreaks:

- Respirator with a HEPA (high-efficiency particulate arrestant) filter, not a dust mask. Wear this only if you have had respirator training and a proper fitting. Dust masks do not provide protection.
- Disposable plastic gloves.
- Goggles or protective eyewear.
- Coveralls or laboratory coats, preferably disposable. Otherwise, you should wear clothes that you don't need to wear all day long, but can change out of and wash as soon as you get home.
- Foot and head covers for very dirty situations.
- Remove coveralls, laboratory coats, and protective gear in a designated "dirty" area. Periodically disinfect nondisposable gear. Wash laboratory coats, coveralls, and other washable items in hot water and bleach.
- Electric fan.
- HEPA filter vacuum cleaner.
- Electrostatic duster.
- Soft cloth.

Dealing with Mold

Deactivating Mold

Mold must be deactivated before we can begin to remove it. The most common options used for deactivating mold are freezing an item or using ultraviolet (UV) lighting. Freezing can be done in-house for small outbreaks or by an outside vendor for large outbreaks. Freeze an item at 0°F or less for at least 72 hours, and the mold should be deactivated. When materials are removed from the freezer, they should be slowly returned to room temperature to prevent condensation on the object, which can reactivate the mold. UV light can also deactivate mold but is damaging to most library, archival, and museum materials, so it should be used with caution. This method should only be used on items with a short lifespan such as magazines and mass-market paperbacks. Never use this method on rare books or items of high value. Place your items under a UV lamp or take your items outdoors on a day when the relative humidity is at 50 percent or lower. Leave materials under the UV lamp or out in the sun for no longer than 30 minutes. Active mold usually changes color and responds within 10 minutes of exposure.

How to Remove Mold from an Item

Before beginning to clean any items, examine the surface carefully for areas of weakness or media that is fragile. Some items will need to be cleaned by a conservator including:

- Charcoal drawings
- Graphite pencil drawings
- Colored pencil drawings
- Water color drawings
- Extremely weak, brittle, or degraded paper
- Documents with deteriorating ink
- Materials that have complex tears or losses

Never attempt to remove mold from a wet item. Wait until the item is dry before attempting to remove mold from it.

How to Remove Mold from the Outside of a Dry Book

Use a HEPA filter vacuum to remove mold growth from the outside of the book. Use a plastic screen held down with weights or a brush attachment covered with cheesecloth or pantyhose to prevent the loss of detached pieces. You can also use either an electrostatic duster or a soft cloth to brush away the mold. For paperback books, use a soft cloth lightly dampened with denatured alcohol to carefully remove the mold. For hardcover books, test an inconspicuous spot first, and then spot-clean with denatured alcohol on a soft cloth.

A brush can also be used to remove mold. Use a soft, wide brush, and carefully brush powdery mold off the surface of the material. This should be done under a fume hood, outside, or the mold should be brushed directly into a vacuum nozzle. Be careful not to rub the mold into the surface, since that will attach it permanently to the cover of a book. Wash the brush thoroughly and often, and discard after use. Yet another option is to use a kneadable eraser. Carefully touch it to the surface and gently lift up. Magic Rub and Staedtler Mars erasers may also be used to softly erase away the mold. When you are erasing, make certain that you are not rubbing the mold into the paper. When you are done, brush the eraser crumbs straight into the garbage bin for prompt removal.

How to Remove Mold from the Pages of a Dry Book

Begin by placing a sheet of silicone release paper or wax paper underneath the moldy page to protect the page behind it. Then use a soft brush to delicately remove any noticeable mold. Finally, dampen a soft cloth with denatured alcohol and carefully remove any remaining mold. As with the cover of a book, you can also use a kneadable eraser to carefully remove mold from the pages of a book.

How to Remove Mold from Textiles and Clothing

If your textiles or historical clothing have a very musty odor to them, it is possible that there may be mold on these items. Inspect the musty-smelling item for visible stains, and then examine those stains under UV lighting. This type of lighting will allow mold stains to shine brighter than the rest of the item. Sometimes an item may have been treated with certain detergents, and the chemicals in those detergents will also shine bright under the UV lighting, so the stain should also be looked at under a microscope to be assured that it is in fact mold. A conservator can also be hired to determine if your textiles have mold.

Once you have determined it is mold, you can begin by vacuuming the textile. A HEPA filter vacuum must be used, and the suction of the vacuum must be gentle and regulated to account for the oftentimes fragile nature of textiles and historical clothing. If vacuuming does not provide you with sufficient results, a textile conservator may be consulted to discuss other options.

SALVAGING FIRE-DAMAGED MATERIALS

If any items in your collection survive a fire, they will usually be damaged in some way. The most common types of fire-related damage are items covered in soot and items that now have a smoky odor.

Removing Soot from a Book

Use a HEPA filter vacuum on a low suction setting to remove as much soot as possible. Then use a soft brush to carefully brush the areas where soot still remains. If soot still remains, a conservator will need to be consulted.

Removing Soot from Textiles and Clothing

Because soot leaves an oily residue, it will be almost impossible to fully remove soot from textiles or clothes without the help of a textile conservator. If you attempt to remove the soot yourself, you should use a HEPA filter vacuum and vacuum the item gently. Do not let the nozzle touch the item; it should be at least an inch away. Do not use any brush attachment that comes with the vacuum, as it tends to push the soot further into the item.

SALVAGING PEST-INFESTED MATERIALS

If you have an insect infestation, do not attempt to use any aerosols or bug bombs, since they have an oil base that will coat materials. If you have a rodent infestation, do not use poison. Poison allows for the possibility of the rodent dying in a place you are unable to get to, causing unpleasant smells and becoming a health hazard. Use traps instead.

Removing Insects from Items

You have three methods to choose from when it comes to removing insects from your collection items: freeze, choke, or fry. Freezing is most widely used. Choking has some risks but can also be used. Frying has been used on collections before, but it is not recommended.

Freezing is the most common method used because it poses no health risks to the library staff or most library materials. Take the infested material and place it in a sealed plastic bag to prevent insects from escaping. If the item is particularly large, you can place it in a box instead, but the box must be sealed. Freeze items at 20 to 0 F for at least 72 hours. Then let the item slowly reach room temperature. After the item has been thawed, you may use a soft brush combined with a HEPA filter vacuum to brush away the dead insects.

Anoxic methods (aka "choking") can also be used to remove insects from items. The way this process works is, in a sealed environment, there is a decrease in oxygen, an increase in carbon dioxide, and the use of inert gases, primarily nitrogen. It is usually done in a traditional fumigation chamber, portable fumigation bubble, or low-permeability bags. While there appears to be no obvious damage to collections, little research has been done on long-term effects. In addition, there is potential danger to staff from exposure to high levels of carbon dioxide, if that is used.

Frying is a method where collection items are treated with heat. While extreme heat has been known to kill insects, it can also cause irreparable harm to the collection items; book pages and covers can scorch and adhesives can soften, causing pages to detach from their bindings in certain books. For this reason, this method is not recommended.

WHEN AN ITEM MIGHT NOT BE SALVAGEABLE

While we hope to be able to save all of our items after a disaster, there are some times when an item is simply not salvageable. There are three main reasons an item should be considered unsalvageable:

If the cost or time is not worth it: Certain items such as periodicals or widely available paperbacks can be discarded and replaced. The time spent on salvaging these items is too much when compared to the low cost to simply replace them.

If it is contaminated: When we have water-damaged materials, the water on those materials can come from a variety of sources. Items can be wet from clean water, rain water, sea water, or a sewage pipe. If your item is wet with contaminated water, this item should be left for a professional conservator to handle or should be replaced if it is more economically feasible.

If it has mold: Some molds are toxic and require the services of a costly professional to clean. Even nontoxic mold can cause allergic reactions in certain people and can be time-consuming to thoroughly clean up. There is also the chance of mold breakouts recurring if mold is not removed completely. Unless the materials in question are of extremely high value, consider disposing of the items and replacing them instead.

This chapter provided the step-by-step procedures for salvaging items in your collection from water damage, mold damage, fire and smoke damage, and pest damage. Utilizing these procedures will increase the likelihood of successful salvage of damaged objects in the library's collection. Knowing when an item may not be salvageable was also discussed in this chapter to better understand that sometimes an object may simply not be salvageable and these losses are to be expected. The next chapter will focus on how to properly prepare for a disaster with staff drills and exercises.

NOTES

1. "Freezing and Drying Wet Books and Records." Northeast Document Conservation Center. Accessed January 18, 2018. https://www.nedcc.org/free-resources/preservation-leaflets/3.-emergency-management/3.12-freezing-and-drying-wet-books-and-records.

2. Tremain, David. "Notes on Emergency Drying of Coated Papers Damaged by Water." Conservation OnLine. Accessed January 18, 2018. http://cool.conservation-us.org/byauth/tremain/coated.html.

3. "Baltimore Academic Libraries Consortium Disaster Preparedness Plan." Disaster Mitigation. Accessed January 18, 2018. http://resources.conservation-us.org/disaster/baltimore-academic-libraries-consortium-disaster-preparedness-plan/.

4. "Emergency Salvage of Wet Books and Records." Northeast Document Conservation Center. Accessed January 18, 2018. https://www.nedcc.org/free-resources/preservation-leaflets/3.-emergency-management/3.6-emergency-salvage-of-wet-books-and-records.

5. "Comparison of Drying Techniques." National Archives and Records Administration. August 15, 2016. Accessed January 18, 2018. https://www.archives.gov/preservation/disaster-response/drying-techniques.html.

6. Ibid.

SOURCES CONSULTED

Dartmouth College Library. "A Simple Book Repair Manual: Air Drying Wet Books." http://www.dart
  mouth.edu/~library/preservation/repair/airdry.html?mswitch-redir=classic.

National Parks Service. "Conserve-O-Grams." Accessed July 5, 2018. https://www.nps.gov/museum/
  publications/conserveogram/cons_toc.html#collectionpreservation.

University of Delaware Library. "How to Dry a Wet Book." Accessed July 5, 2018. http://www2.lib.udel
  .edu/Preservation/wet_books.htm.

DATE	CALL NUMBER/ ACCESSION NUMBER/ ID NUMBER	TITLE	OVERALL CONDITION	EVALUATED BY
List the date of evaluation here	List the call number, accession number, or other identification number here	List the title of the item here	List the overall condition of the item here as well as the location and description of damage	List the name of the person who evaluated the item here

Figure 5.1   Salvage Condition Report Form

CALL NUMBER/ ACCESSION NUMBER	TITLE	FORMAT	CURRENT LOCATION
Enter the call number, accession number, or other identification number here	Enter the title of the object here	List the format of the item here.	List the item's current location
025.84 P933 2015	*Preserving Our Heritage: Perspectives from Antiquity to the Digital Age*	Book	Salvage Area #1
MA 05.2	*Carol Neaves' Jaycee Scrapbook*	Scrapbook	Salvage Area #2

Figure 5.2 Salvage Relocation Form

CHAPTER 6

Staff Training: Exercises and Drills

Part of being prepared for a disaster is practicing what you will do when a disaster occurs. This means that the disaster team should regularly be doing training exercises and practice drills for the disasters that are most likely to occur at your institution. This chapter will provide you with some training exercises and practice drills; you should include the most relevant exercises and drills in your disaster plan. Commit to completing the exercises described here and engaging in the practice drills once or twice a year.

GETTING STARTED

The exercises are designed to be completed with the disaster team and any other relevant parties, ideally in a meeting room or anywhere that is conducive to verbal interaction with the other team members. The exercises are different from the practice drills in that the exercises will be all "talk," while the drills will be more "action." In other words, the exercises are discussion-based events where the disaster team discusses what actions the team members would take during a specific disaster-related event, while the practice drills will have the disaster team members performing their roles in a simulated environment.

For the exercises, divide everyone into the following roles: facilitator, disaster team members, and observers. The facilitator will be the one prompting questions and moderating the discussion. The team leader can take on this role if no one outside the disaster team is available. The disaster team members will be the ones answering the questions asked of them by the facilitator. They will be responsible for general knowledge–type questions and questions that are specific to their role on the disaster team. You may also have observers involved in your exercises. They will not directly participate in the exercise, but they can ask follow-up questions or they can provide additional insight, if desired. It is up to you to decide how much input you want from your observers.

The facilitator should ask all the participants to introduce themselves, state their position in the library, and their role in the disaster team. After the introductions, the facilitator should stress that the purpose of the exercises is to identify strengths and weaknesses of the current disaster plan and to strengthen the library's ability to handle disaster situations. The facilitator will choose an exercise or multiple exercises and read out the scenario. The team members will try to do their best to answer the discussion questions as a group, and they should refer to the disaster plan if they are not 100 percent sure of the answer.

The practice drills will include whoever is named as facilitator, the disaster team, and any observers. The facilitator will be responsible for starting the simulated event and timing it as well. The disaster team members will be responsible for going through their roles as if an actual disaster or emergency were occurring. The observers should not directly get involved in the practice drill, but they should observe and take notes, which should be discussed after the practice drill.

After each exercise or drill, the disaster team should write up a report that reviews how that exercise or drill went. Be sure to include what was well done, what needs improvement, and if any changes should be made to the disaster plan.

WATER-RELATED DISASTERS

Exercise #1: Water Damage via Flooding

Scenario: Sometime between the library closing last night and this morning, the nearby river overflowed and water entered into the library. An inventory of the collection finds that 100 items have suffered water damage. They consist of:

- Leather-bound books (slightly wet)
- Paperback books (extremely wet)
- DVDs (moderately wet)

Discussion Questions:

1. Does the salvage coordinator know the immediate steps to take (within the first 24–48 hours)?

2. Does the operations coordinator know his or her role in this scenario?
3. Does the documentations coordinator know his or her role in this situation?

Exercise #2: Water Damage via Structural Damage

Scenario: A pipe has burst in the basement. By the time the staff have been notified, there is already 6 inches of water flooding the basement floor.

Discussion Questions:

1. Discuss immediate procedures.
2. Discuss evacuation procedures. Will we evacuate the building? Will we block access only to the affected area? Look into your evacuation procedures for the answer.

MOLD OUTBREAK

Exercise #1

Scenario: A patron returns a book, and you notice what appears to be mold on the book.

Discussion Questions:

1. Does the disaster team know what to do immediately? The disaster team should know that an item like this should be placed in a sealable plastic bag and isolated from the rest of the collection.
2. Does the disaster team know how to identify mold? Everyone on the disaster team should be aware of what mold looks like. They should also know whom to call to determine if the mold is toxic.

Exercise #2

Scenario: You are helping to locate a book for a patron, and when you find it, you notice that the book has what appears to be mold. As you look at the books nearby, you notice that they also have mold. In fact, the whole shelf contains books where mold appears to be present.

Discussion Questions:

1. Since this scenario has multiple books affected, does the disaster team know what the immediate response should be in this situation? They should know to block off the area with affected materials and find the source for the mold outbreak (check the temperature, relative humidity, check for leaks, etc.)

2. Is the disaster team aware of the dangers of mold? Ask them to discuss the danger mold provides to the building, the collection, and to the patrons and staff.

PEST OUTBREAK

Exercise #1: Possible Rodent Infestation

Scenario: As you are walking to the storage area, you notice what appear to be mouse droppings.

Discussion Question:

1. What is the immediate response to seeing possible mouse droppings? The disaster team should know how to implement integrated pest management strategies in this scenario. This means that they should know that traps should be set and monitored. They should know where to locate the pest trap log form and how to properly complete the form.

Exercise #2: Insect Infestation

Scenario: While pulling a book for a patron, you notice what appears to be [choose an insect] damage to a book.

Discussion Questions:

1. Does the disaster team know how to identify [choose an insect] damage? They should be able to identify this particular type of damage or know how to find out by either looking up the signs in a book or an authoritative website or conversing with a colleague who may know how to identify the different types of insect damage.
2. Does the disaster team know how to mitigate a [choose an insect] infestation? They should know all the environmental conditions that allow [chose an insect] to thrive and how to correct the situation.

THEFT IN THE LIBRARY

Exercise #1: Theft

Scenario: You work in the reading room of the special collections department of the library. A researcher requests a rare book, but when you go to retrieve the book, you notice that it is missing from the storage area.

Discussion Questions:

1. Does the disaster team know how to report a book theft? Everyone should know whom to contact within the library to report a book theft, and if the book is of high value, a police report should be filed. The communications coordinator should also know how to report a theft to local book dealers and the International League of Antiquarian Book Sellers.
2. Does the disaster team know how to locate who may have had the book last? There should be a record of who had the book last, and there should be a photocopy of this person's personal identification card. These items should be pulled and given to authorities to help with the case.

BOMB THREAT

Exercise #1: Bomb Threat

Scenario: During operating hours, a bomb threat is called in. The caller says the bomb is located in [pick a location in your library] and will go off in one hour.

Discussion Question:

1. Discuss the first actions. Does everyone on the disaster team know how to use the bomb threat form? Do they know where to access the form?

Exercise #2: Bomb Explosion

Scenario: During operating hours, a bomb explodes in [pick a location in your library]. At the time of the explosion, five patrons were in the location, and one has been critically hurt by the explosion. Residents and business nearby begin approaching the library to see what has happened. A reporter with a camera crew arrives shortly after.

Discussion Questions:

1. Does the disaster team know what to do immediately after an explosion?
2. Does the disaster team know what to do about the critically injured patron?
3. Does the communications coordinator know how to handle the people outside as well as the reporter and camera crew?

HURRICANES

Exercise #1: Hurricane Watch

Scenario: A hurricane watch has been issued during operating hours.

Discussion Questions:

1. Does the disaster team know the difference between a hurricane watch and a warning? Discuss the differences with the team, and make sure everyone is aware of the differences between these two terms.
2. When will we notify staff and patrons? How? Discuss when you have to alert the staff and when you have to alert the patrons of the library as well as how you plan on doing it (i.e., an announcement over the speaker system, a text message, e-mail, verbal delivery in person, etc.).
3. Should we begin to move vulnerable items to a safe space? Based on the salvage priority list, decide if and when you will move your most valuable items to safety. In some cases, it may be prudent to move items away from windows (place the items on tables in an interior location) or take items off the bottom shelves.
4. Is there any preparation we can do now before the hurricane occurs? Have the team discuss what preparation can be done when a hurricane watch is issued.

Exercise #2: Hurricane Warning

Scenario: A hurricane warning has been issued during operating hours.

Discussion Questions:

1. Does the disaster team know the difference between a hurricane watch and a warning? Discuss the differences with the team, and make sure everyone is aware of the differences between these two terms.
2. When will we notify staff and patrons? How? Discuss when you have to alert the staff and when you have to alert the patrons of the library as well as how you plan on doing it (i.e., an announcement over the speaker system, a text message, e-mail, verbal delivery in person, etc.). Because we are dealing with a disaster warning, text message and e-mails might not be read in time. If you do send out a text message or e-mail, make sure that you also deliver the information in person or via a speaker system.
3. If the hurricane should occur, does the disaster team know the location where staff and patrons will go to be safe from harm? Have the

disaster team consult the disaster plan to look at evacuation procedures and safe spaces in the event of a hurricane occurring.
4. If we have time, should we begin to move vulnerable items to a safe space? Staff and patrons are your top priority. If they are all safe and you still have time to safely relocate your priority items, will you do so?

TORNADOES

Exercise #1: Tornado Watch

Scenario: A tornado watch has been issued during operating hours.

Discussion Questions:

1. Does the disaster team know the difference between a tornado watch and a warning? Discuss the differences with the team, and make sure everyone is aware of the differences between these two terms.
2. When will we notify staff and patrons? How? Discuss when you have to alert the staff and when you have to alert the patrons of the library as well as how you plan on doing it (i.e., an announcement over the speaker system, a text message, e-mail, verbal delivery in person, etc.).
3. Should we begin to move vulnerable items to a safe space? Based on the salvage priority list, decide if and when you will move your most valuable items to safety.
4. Is there any preparation we can do know before the tornado occurs?

Exercise #2: Tornado Warning

Scenario: A tornado warning has been issued during operating hours.

Discussion Questions:

1. Does the disaster team know the difference between a tornado watch and a warning? Discuss the differences with the team, and make sure everyone is aware of the differences between these two terms.
2. When will we notify staff and patrons? How? Discuss when you have to alert the staff and when you have to alert the patrons of the library as well as how you plan on doing it (i.e., an announcement over the speaker system, a text message, e-mail, verbal delivery in person, etc.). Because we are dealing with a disaster warning, text messages and e-mails might not be read in time. If you do send out a text message or e-mail, make sure that you also deliver the information in person or via a speaker system.

3. If the tornado should occur, does the disaster team know the location where staff and patrons will go to be safe from harm? Have the disaster team consult the disaster plan to look at evacuation procedures and safe spaces in the event of a tornado occurring.
4. If we have time, should we begin to move vulnerable items to a safe space? Staff and patrons are your top priority. If they are all safe and you still have time to safely relocate your priority items, will you do so?

Exercise #3: Tornado Occurrence Exercise

Scenario: A tornado has touched down during operating hours. The power in the library is out.

Discussion Questions:

1. Does the disaster team know what to do when a tornado has touched down? The disaster team should know what to do immediately following a tornado occurrence. These procedures should be memorized; there may be no time to find the disaster plan workbook on the shelf or to pull up a digital copy of the disaster plan. Another reason these procedures need to be memorized is that if the power goes out (like it has in this exercise), you won't be able to pull up a digital copy of your disaster plan, and the physical copy might also be hard to find if the sun has set and there is no light.
2. How will we communicate with no power? You will need to have a back-up communication system that does not rely on electricity. Battery-powered walkie-talkies or two-way radios are good options. While some may decide that cell phones may be another option, you should consider that cell phone towers might be down and cell phones may not be able to be recharged.

Tornado Practice Drill:

Step 1: Start the tornado drill by announcing that this is a tornado drill but that all participants should act as though a tornado warning has actually been issued.

Step 2: The disaster team members should evacuate everyone just as they would during a real tornado warning. Use stairs to reach the lowest level of a building; avoid using elevators.

Step 3: Once participants reach the designated safe area, they should crouch as low as possible to the floor, facing down and covering their heads with their hands.

Step 4: Once everyone has evacuated and taken cover, announce that the drill is now over.

Step 5: The disaster team should review how the tornado drill went and discuss ways for improvement.

EARTHQUAKES

Exercise #1: Earthquake Occurrence

Scenario: The library is open when an earthquake occurs.

Discussion Question:

1. What is the immediate response to an earthquake? Does the disaster team know what to do when an actual earthquake occurs? Do they know where to evacuate people to? Do they know the best places to be in the building during an earthquake?

Exercise #2: Earthquake Aftermath

Scenario: Before the library opened, there was an earthquake. You have arrived at the building, and when you open the doors, you see collapsed stacks and what appears to be roof damage.

Discussion Question:

1. Does the disaster team know whom to call in this situation? Do they know whether they should enter the building at this point or not? Do they know what to do when patrons start to arrive?

    This chapter is an excellent resource for the regular training of the library staff. Practice drills and exercises have been provided for common types of disasters and emergencies. Training should be done on a regular basis to ensure the success of effective response to a disaster. The next chapter will center on technology and the disaster plan.

CHAPTER 7

Technology Tools

As technology has advanced, more and more libraries are finding themselves with vast digital collections, which also must be protected from disaster. In this chapter, you will learn how to use your disaster plan to protect your digital collections. Technology has also given us great options to use along with our disaster plan to make it more comprehensive. In this chapter, you will learn how to protect your digital objects and the ways we can use technology to complement our disaster plan.

Just as you assessed risks to your physical collection, you will also assess risks to your digital collection. Begin by taking an inventory of your digital collections, and ask the following questions:

- Is this object created in a standard file format?
- Do multiple copies exist of this digital object?
- Is there a digital preservation plan in place for this object?

If you answered yes to all these questions, then your digital collections are at a low risk of being lost or damaged beyond repair. If you answered no to all of these questions, then your digital collections are at a high risk of being lost forever.

Next, have a look at the technology used to maintain the digital collections, and ask the following questions:

- Is your hardware stored properly?
- Is regularly scheduled maintenance performed on your hardware?
- Is the hardware used in secure locations only?
- Is your software up to date?
- Are files password-protected as necessary?

If you answered yes to all these questions, then your hardware and software are at a low risk of being lost or damaged beyond repair. If you answered no to all of these questions, then your technology infrastructure is at a high risk of failing and causing damage to your digital objects.

Now that a risk assessment has been completed of the library's digital objects and related technology, you must figure out ways to minimize risks. For digital files that were created on nonstandard file formats, try to have them reformatted to more standard file formats. The more standard the format is, the more likely the associated software will be available to open the file. For digital objects that have only one copy, you will want to create multiple copies and you will want these copies in various locations. The more copies you have and the more places in which they are located, it means that if one copy is damaged, you still have other copies around, so this digital object can persevere. If you do not have a digital preservation plan, the chances of your digital collection lasting in the long run are very slim at best. A digital preservation plan ensures that digital objects can be accessed in the present and in the future. Hardware also needs to be protected from damage. Hardware should always be stored properly, so be careful to learn the best location to place the hardware and be sure to avoid areas that are not recommended, such as areas close to heat sources or windows. Having regularly scheduled maintenance can allow for early detection of hardware problems and provide ample time to have them fixed. Ensuring that your hardware is used in secure locations only (such as offices that have a locked entry) makes sure that the occurrence of hardware theft is minimized. Software should always be checked to ensure that it is up to date. Old versions of software could cause access issues. Password protection is an absolute necessity for certain digital objects. Digital objects that are sensitive in nature should be password-protected to prevent unwanted access by certain parties.

In addition to protecting technology, let us look at how we can use technology in combination with our disaster plan. In the next part of this chapter, we will discuss the best apps, databases, and other technology tools that you can use to create a more comprehensive disaster plan. It should be noted that the majority of the items mentioned are not intended for replacing certain portions of your disaster plan manual; they are only meant to complement or enhance the value of your physical manual. For obvious reasons, it would be foolish to rely solely on technology during a disaster.

GENERAL DISASTER-RELATED TECHNOLOGY TOOLS

Tech Tool: dPlan (www.dplan.org)

Cost: Free

Features: This online tool simplifies the process of writing a disaster plan for your library. It offers an in-depth fill-in-the-blank template into which you enter information about your organization. Based on the information you enter, dPlan then produces a printed disaster plan specific to your library.

Tech Tool: ERS: Emergency Response and Salvage (Mobile App)

Operating System: Android, iOS

Cost: Free

Features: This app is based on the Heritage Preservation's Emergency Response and Salvage Wheel, and it offers practical salvage tips for 11 types of collections: books and paper, ceramics, electronic records, framed art, furniture, metal, natural history, organics, photographs, stones, and textiles.

Tech Tool: Disaster Alert by Pacific Disaster Center (Mobile and Web App)

Operating System: Android, iOS, can also use web-based platform

Cost: Free

Features: The very detailed Disaster Alert allows you to view various types of disasters occurring globally or locally; track alerts for hurricanes, cyclones, earthquakes, and floods; and much more. You also have the option on receiving automatic updates to specific disasters.

Tech Tool: First Aid by American Red Cross (Mobile App)

Operating System: Android, iOS

Cost: Free

Features: First Aid has simple step-by-step instructions to guide the user through everyday first aid scenarios. This app is fully integrated with 911, so the user can call at any time. There are also educational videos and safety tips within this app to help protect you in various disasters. The content in this app is preloaded, which means users have instant access to all of the described information at any time, even without reception or an Internet connectivity.

Tech Tool: Panic Mate (Mobile App)

Operating System: Android

Cost: Free

Features: Create an emergency contact list in this app, and then with the press of a button, you can notify those contacts that you are in trouble. This is a great app for the disaster team members to use when a disaster occurs during operating hours and you want to be able to keep tabs on everyone's location and safety. When you press the panic button, your emergency contacts receive an e-mail and/or text message alerting them that you are in trouble along with your current location. This app also has a callback button, which you can use when you need someone to phone you back.

FLOOD-RELATED TECHNOLOGY TOOLS

Tech Tool: Floodwatch (Mobile App)
Operating System: iOS
Cost: Free
Features: Floodwatch allows users to monitor rivers and streams throughout the United States. This app displays both recent and historical river heights, precipitation totals, and flood stage information. Graphs are available to help the user visualize the rise and fall of the river.

Tech Tool: Flood by American Red Cross (Mobile App)
Operating System: Android, iOS
Cost: Free
Features: This app will tell the user the difference between a flood warning and a flood watch and has an "I'm Safe" notification, which is sharable through social media, text, and e-mail. It also has an audible siren that automatically goes off even if the app is closed when the National Oceanic and Atmospheric Administration (NOAA) issues a flood warning. The content in this app is preloaded, which means users have instant access to all of the described information at any time, even without reception or an Internet connectivity.

MOLD- AND PEST-RELATED TECHNOLOGY TOOLS

Tech Tool: Mold 101: Health and Safety (Mobile App)
Operating System: Android, iOS
Cost: Free
Features: This app will tell you how to identify mold; precautions you should take when dealing with mold; and work practices, procedures, and methods for mold removal and cleanup. This app is geared toward small-scale mold cleanup.

Tech Tool: Museum Pests (https://museumpests.net/)
Cost: Free
Features: Museum Pests offers an extensive image library, which you can search through to see images of common insects and rodents. Museum Pests also offers guidance on prevention and monitoring of pests.

MEDICAL EMERGENCY–RELATED TOOLS

Tech Tool: ICE Standard (Mobile App)
Operating System: Android, iOS
Cost: Free
Features: This app allows you to enter your emergency contacts, medical conditions, allergies, and medications you are taking. The library should encourage both their staff and patrons to download and utilize this app. Having this information handy when a person becomes unconscious or incapacitated in some way can be lifesaving.

FIRE-RELATED TECHNOLOGY TOOLS

Tech Tool: CAL FIRE Ready for Wildfire (Mobile App)
Operating System: Android, iOS
Cost: Free
Features: With this app, the user can get alerts when a wildfire is reported in a chosen zip code or within 30 miles of the user. You can also use this app to stay updated about current wildfires including viewing a map of all current fires. This app also provides the user with informational videos about wildfire preparation and prevention.

LIBRARY THEFT PREVENTION–RELATED TECHNOLOGY TOOL

Tech Tool: Stolen Books (www.stolen-book.org)
Cost: Free
Features: This database is run by the International League of Antiquarian Booksellers, and it contains a list of all books reported stolen after 2010. You can use this database to list your stolen books in the hope that booksellers will look here first before purchasing a book from a book thief.

ACTIVE SHOOTER–RELATED TECHNOLOGY TOOL

Tech Tool: Active Shooter Response by TRADOC Mobile (Mobile App)
Operating System: Android, iOS
Cost: Free
Features: Created by the U.S. Army, this app provides ready access to information and guidelines on preparing, responding, and managing active shooter situations. There is also training information, and a feature to call 911 is built into the app.

HURRICANE-RELATED TECHNOLOGY TOOLS

Tech Tool: Hurricane Hound (Mobile App)
Operating System: Android
Cost: $1.99
Features: Hurricane Hound uses Google Maps to track forecasts and locations of Atlantic and East Pacific hurricanes and tropical storms. This app also points out areas the National Weather Service is watching.

Tech Tool: Hurricane Tracker (Mobile App)
Operating System: Android, iOS
Cost: $2.99
Features: This mobile app offers detailed threat level and radar maps; National Hurricane Center updates; video forecast updates; and real-time alerts for hurricanes, tropical storms, tropical depressions, and invests.

Tech Tool: Hurricane by American Red Cross (Mobile App)
Operating System: Android, iOS
Cost: Free
Features: This mobile app tracks and forecasts the hurricanes; explains how to make and execute an emergency plan; and how to use social media, text, or e-mail to tell others you are safe during and after a storm.

TORNADO-RELATED TECHNOLOGY TOOLS

Tech Tool: Tornado by Red Cross (Mobile App)
Operating System: Android, iOS
Cost: Free
Features: Use this app for basic tornado information. Tornado app has weather radar and a guide to help you prepare, listing resources to keep on hand, items to keep in an emergency kit, and the locations of nearby shelters. This app has an audible siren that automatically goes off even if the app is closed when NOAA issues a tornado warning. The content in this app is preloaded, which means users have instant access to all of the described information at any time, even without reception or an Internet connectivity.

Tech Tool: TornadoSpy+ (Mobile App)
Operating System: iOS
Cost: $2.99
Features: This app sends alerts and shows weather on radar maps. It also lets users upload crowdsourced information about tornadoes and other dangerous weather in their areas. The makers of this

app say that in 2013 an Oklahoma City tornado was reported on the TornadoSpy+ app 20 minutes before the NOAA reported it, allowing the users of this app more time to protect themselves than those not using TornadoSpy+.[1]

EARTHQUAKE-RELATED TECHNOLOGY TOOLS

Tech Tool: Earthquake by the American Red Cross (Mobile App)
Operating System: Android, iOS
Cost: Free
Features: This app comes with instructions to let the user know what to do before, during, and after earthquakes or tsunamis, even if the user has no data or Internet connectivity. Earthquake will send the user notifications and alerts when a quake occurs. This app also provides an illustrated history of earthquakes in the user's area and maps with recent quakes throughout the world.

Tech Tool: Earthquake Network (Mobile App)
Operating System: Android
Cost: Free
Features: Earthquake Network allows you to receive real-time notifications of the earthquakes detected by the network. It allows other users to manually report an earthquake, and you are then able to see a map of all the user reports in real time. Users can also receive the notifications of the earthquakes detected by the United States Geological Survey (USGS) and European Mediterranean Seismological Centre (EMSC). Other features of this app include automatically sending emergency text messages and e-mails to a list of contacts and the ability to chat with other people during an earthquake emergency.

This chapter has provided guidelines for risk assessment of a library's digital collection and ways to mitigate damage to digital objects and related technological infrastructure. In addition, this chapter has examined the best technology tools that can enhance your disaster plan. The next chapter will review everything we have learned about creating a disaster plan and discuss what to do after your disaster plan is complete.

NOTE

1. Justin Time. "TornadoSpy: Tornado Maps, Warnings and Alerts on the App Store." App Store. January 12, 2011. Accessed January 20, 2018. https://itunes.apple.com/us/app/tornadospy-tornado-maps-warnings-and-alerts/id413928923?mt=8.

CHAPTER 8

After the Disaster Plan

After the disaster plan is complete, the work is not over just yet. For your disaster plan to be truly effective, you will need to follow this workflow cycle: prepare, respond, recover, and evaluate (Figure 8.1).

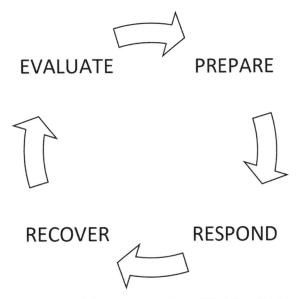

Figure 8.1   Disaster Preparedness Workflow Cycle

131

DISASTER PREPAREDNESS WORKFLOW CYCLE

Prepare

Preparing is the most important thing the disaster team can do. Preparing means assessing and minimizing risks, acquiring the proper supplies, and practicing for a disaster. The risk assessment coordinator should constantly be assessing risks. Things that might not have been considered a risk when you first created your disaster plan may now be a concern. The disaster team members should always be thinking how they can minimize these risks. In addition to your physical collections, be sure to also assess the risk of your digital collections. The communications coordinator should prepare with mock interview exercises to be undertaken at least once or twice a year and be prepared to communicate effectively during a disaster using all the communication tools available to him or her including holding statement templates and disaster notification scripts. Becoming familiar with disaster notification scripts, how to write a press release, and how to communicate with the press and media is part of being prepared. The operations coordinator will also need to make sure that your library has the proper supplies as discussed in Chapter 5 to handle high-risk situations, and it is important to keep track of those supplies and replenish as necessary. The last thing you want during a disaster is to realize you do not have the emergency supplies needed because the supplies were not replenished after the last disaster. The salvage coordinator should be well versed in salvage techniques and should practice these techniques periodically. A great way to do this is to put aside some items that the library is throwing out and practice on those. Finally, being prepared means you are regularly practicing what to do in the event that a disaster occurs. As discussed previously, practice comes in the form of tabletop exercises and practice drills. Whenever your team completes a tabletop exercise or a practice drill, you will have to review what you have learned, and if applicable, update the disaster plan.

Respond

If you are properly prepared, then responding to a disaster should be a relatively calm procedure with a minimum of stress. Your disaster team members should know their roles and the actions they have to carry out. If you have been practicing regularly, your team members may have their roles memorized. If not, pull out the disaster plan manual—that is what it is there for. Remember that the disaster plan should be easy to locate; there should be multiple copies in multiple formats; there should be a table of contents so that the needed information can be accessed quickly; and it should be written in a clear and concise manner—an emergency or disaster is no time for flowery language. How effectively you respond to a disaster will be determined by how effective your disaster plan is.

Recover

Because there is a small window for successful recovery of your library's materials, you need to make sure that your salvage priority list is up to date and the instructions for the proper salvage techniques are on hand for your salvage coordinator. Salvage instructions should be easy to read in a step-by-step format. If things get too complicated for the salvage coordinator, you should have the contact information of a preservation specialist or conservator, who may be called in to handle the situation. The recovery of the library building will be dependent on how quickly you respond to the disaster. Part of recovery is becoming operational again, so if your library has suffered extensive structural damage and needs to be closed for repairs, you should have a space where you can temporarily set up your library, or you should have an agreement with another library to allow your patrons access to their materials. The communications coordinator should stay in contact with the patrons, informing them of the current state of the library, what they can do to access materials while the library is recovering, and when the library is expected to be fully operational.

Evaluate

After the library is operational and salvage has been completed, a post-disaster evaluation form should be filled out. This form will describe the incident and the damage to the building and the collection and will list what you did well, where you could improve for next time, and what will be the timeline to make those improvements. An evaluation of every aspect of the disaster plan and the disaster team's response would include several items. First evaluate whether the disaster plan met the needs of the disaster team during the disaster. The team should explain if certain emergency procedures were not clear enough or specific enough. If the amount of emergency supplies was not sufficient, this should also be discussed. After this, the team itself should be evaluated. Each disaster team member should evaluate himself or herself and rate how well he or she was able to fulfill his or her team role. The disaster team leader should provide feedback to each team member as well. Based on these evaluations, the team will address all the ways in which the disaster plan can be improved and set an estimated time frame for working on those issues. After the evaluation step, you will find yourself right back at the beginning, preparing for your next disaster. This book has included the basic steps to follow for your workflow. If you follow this workflow, you will find that after each disaster, your disaster team has grown better-equipped to handle any future incidents.

Type of Disaster	
Date of Incident	
Time of Incident	

Describe Damage to the Building

Describe Damage to the Collection

Improvements Needed to the Disaster Plan

Improvements Needed to the Disaster Team

Improvements Timeline

Figure 8.2   Overall Evaluation Form

Name	
Disaster Team Role	
Date of Incident	

How well did you feel you fulfilled your disaster team role?

What areas of your role did you feel most confident in?

What areas do you feel you could improve upon?

What do you feel is needed for you to improve upon your weakest areas?

Disaster Team Leader Feedback

Figure 8.3 Disaster Team Evaluation Form

ANNOTATED BIBLIOGRAPHY

Dadson, Emma. *Emergency Planning and Response for Libraries, Archives, and Museums.* Blue Ridge Summit, PA: Scarecrow Press, 2014.

    Accredited disaster recovery specialist Emma Dadson is the author of this very detailed book on planning and responding to emergencies. Geared toward librarians, archivists, and museum professionals, this work is a straightforward and comprehensive resource for emergency planning. Topics include the roles and responsibilities of the emergency management team, what to include in your response kit, and proper salvage procedures for collections. The case studies offered in the book are helpful for understanding real-world applications of a disaster plan.

Heritage Preservation. *Field Guide to Emergency Response: A Vital Tool for Cultural Institutions.* Washington, DC: Heritage Preservation, 2006.

    Though over a decade old, this work written by Heritage Preservation provides valuable information on responding to an emergency. Written in a format that is easily comprehendible by those with little to no experience in emergency management, this book is divided into four sections: what to do first, the response team, top ten problems to expect, and resources. Included with the book is a helpful instructional DVD as well as a disaster supplies shopping list.

Kahn, Miriam B. *Disaster Response and Planning for Libraries.* 3rd ed. Chicago: American Library Association, 2012.

    The third edition of this book by consultant, author, and teacher Miriam B. Kahn introduces us to disaster planning. This book is for those with little to no experience in the area. Beginning with the response phase and then moving on to recovery, prevention, and creating a disaster plan, the book is a straightforward, easy read. In addition, this book's appendix contains helpful checklists and forms to aid in your disaster planning as well as a list of disaster-related vendors to keep on hand.

Mallery, Mary. *Technology Disaster Response and Recovery Planning.* London: Facet Publishing, 2015.

    Written by various professionals specializing in preservation and disaster-related issues and edited by Mary Mallery, associate dean for technical services at Montclair State University, this book addresses disaster-related concerns specific to technology. Topics include risk assessment for digital collections, planning and executing a response to a digital disaster, and cloud computing and disaster mitigation. Of particular interest are the case studies in the second part of this book, which provide examples of real-life scenarios as well as lessons learned from each incident.

Robertson, Guy. *Disaster Planning for Libraries: Process and Guidelines.* Waltham, MA: Elsevier/Chandos Publishing, 2015.

    As a developer of disaster plans and training programs for various organizations and institutions, Guy Robertson expertly provides guidelines on how to create a disaster plan based on his experience as a bibliographer and rare book specialist. Throughout the book, interviews with library administrators working in different libraries across the world provide an assortment of perspectives on how to prepare for a disaster. The highlights of this work are the chapters on orientation and training programs and basic tabletop exercises for library staff.

Todaro, Julie. *Emergency Preparedness for Libraries.* Lanham, MD: Government Institutes, 2009.

    This work by dean of library services at Austin (Texas) Community College and former president of American Library Association (ALA) Julie Todaro brings to light various library management skills with procedures and measures for mitigating emergencies and planning. Todaro's book equips library staff with comprehensive procedures for safeguarding the library facilities, the library personnel, and the patrons, including the pre-disaster steps and procedures, the process and personnel to be included in an emergency action plan, ways of converting written plans practically in real-life situations, safety precautions to be employed when caring for those affected by an emergency in a library, and the kind of information to be released to the media and within the organization after a disaster.

INDEX

ABOUT THE AUTHOR

Carmen Cowick is the director of preservation services at Preserve This, where she provides training, support, and consulting services for libraries in the areas of preservation and collections care. She received a bachelor's degree in art history and a master's degree in library science with a certificate in archives and preservation of cultural materials from CUNY Queens College in New York City. Cowick has had several articles published in peer-reviewed journals and has given presentations at both regional and national professional conferences on preservation and collections care topics. She is coauthor of the book chapter "Planning for a Disaster: Effective Emergency Management in the 21st Century," in *Handbook of Research on Disaster Management and Contingency Planning in Modern Libraries*.